QUANTITATIVE METHODS

Crucial Study Guides for Business Degree Courses

Titles in the series

Financial Accounting	ISBN 1 903337 00 3	Price £9.99
Business Information Systems	ISBN 1 903337 01 1	Price £9.99
Microeconomics	ISBN 1 903337 02 X	Price £9.99
Business Law	ISBN 1 903337 03 8	Price £9.99
Organisational Behaviour	ISBN 1 903337 04 6	Price £9.99
Quantitative Methods	ISBN 1 903337 05 4	Price £9.99

To order, please contact our distributors:

Plymbridge Distributors, Estover Road, Plymouth, PL6 7PY
Tel: 01752 202301. Fax: 01752 202333. Email: orders@plymbridge.com.
www.plymbridge.com

QUANTITATIVE METHODS

Stewart MacLeod and Gordon Ferrier

First published in 2002 by Crucial, a division of Learning Matters Ltd.

British Library Cataloguing in Publication Data
A CIP record for this book is available from the British Library.

ISBN 1 903337 05 4

Crucial
58 Wonford Road
Exeter EX2 4LQ
Tel: 01392 215560
Email: info@crucial.uk.com
www.crucial.uk.com

Cover design by Topics – The Creative Partnership
Project Management by Deer Park Productions
Typeset by GCS Typesetting, Leighton Buzzard, Beds
Printed and bound in Great Britain by Bell & Bain Ltd, Glasgow

Contents

STUDYING QUANTITATIVE
METHODS AT DEGREE LEVEL

Summary

Quantitative methods is a subject that many students at degree level will be studying even though they did not actively select it as one of their subjects. If you are one of those students, then this study guide has been designed to cater for your particular needs. Students of Business Studies, Accountancy, Marketing, etc. will all have to pass at least one Quantitative Methods examination (or similar), but will then often leave the subject behind as later years of their course focus on the 'core' subjects of the qualification. The same applies to many professional courses, such as those for membership of the Chartered Accountancy institutes.

This chapter gives an introduction to the ways in which you can study successfully for a Quantitative Methods examination at degree or professional level. You will be given advice here on:

- how to use lectures and tutorials effectively;
- how to use textbooks and other resources;
- how to tackle examinations successfully.

Good practice

There are many publications available on the basics of study techniques, covering the use of time, where to study, note taking, etc. We will concentrate here on how to apply best practice in the context of studying Quantitative Methods. If you feel you are unfamiliar with how to approach study at this level, it would be worth checking with your college or university what resources they have. As well as written resources in libraries, etc., many larger institutions will have full-time staff available to give advice on studying and various other aspects of student life. You should also have an advisor or tutor for your course, who you can contact for this kind of advice and support. Make sure you know which members of staff are available to assist you if you need some advice or direction during your course.

Crucial tip	Remember that colleges and universities are large organisations with many students and different courses. You need to be proactive in ensuring that you get off to a good start and maintain good progress in your studies. In many respects, at this level students are left to get on with things and take responsibility for their studies much more than tends to be the case in secondary school.

Section 1   Learning from classes

Classes at degree level can take different formats, from lectures with 100 students held in a huge lecture theatre to tutorial groups of half a dozen students or less. Approaches are changing all the time as the student population has increased, more colleges have become universities, new course are introduced, etc. You may find that your course does not use the terms 'lecture' and 'tutorial', but has classes, seminars, group working, practical sessions, etc. For simplicity, we will use the term 'classes' in this chapter, and where appropriate draw some distinctions between the different size and type of class.

Whatever the type of class, the whole point of them is that you, the student, can learn about the subject being taught. From the beginning, you should approach classes as being one of the key elements of your course and your preparation for an examination. It would be unfortunate to regard classes as **just** a preparation for the examination, as education should be much wider in its purpose. But it would be unrealistic if we tried to ignore the fact that for most students doing Quantitative Methods, passing the examination is by far their greatest priority. So, without trying to overemphasise this role of classes, you should look to take an active attitude in each class. This does mean that you have to keep interrupting the tutor constantly, but it should mean that you can ask yourself the following questions:

- **Do I know what topic the tutor is focusing on and where it fits into my syllabus?** Ideally you should have a clear course plan with dates, topics, syllabus references and textbook references that you can use as a map through the course.
- **Can I distinguish between what is essential to my course/examination and what is peripheral or even an irrelevant digression?** This may be obvious if the tutor is discussing the previous evening's episode of a soap opera, but if she is talking about multiple regression is that because she is fascinated by the topic or because you might get an examination question on it?

- **Have I understood what has been said?** It is easy to fall into the trap of writing down what the tutor says, hoping to read and understand it later. If the only role of the class were to give you a set of notes, a lot of bother could be saved by simply sending a copy of neat notes to every student and cancelling the class.

- **Is my concentration level waning?** Part of the tutor's role should be to make the class interesting and to vary the pace and style to help maintain the students' interest and attention. But you can play your part by being active in terms of paying attention, taking notes, asking/answering questions, applying the teaching to your own experience, etc.

- **Do I know how I will take this forward?** The better tutors will end a class by setting homework, giving reading references, checking that you have all understood the material, etc. But, again, you have some responsibility as well for considering what to do next, and asking for advice from the tutor if necessary. This is particularly important if some of the material has been difficult – do you know how to go about getting more information, doing some wider reading, getting additional examples, or having the opportunity to discuss the topic?

> **Crucial tip**   Classes do not exist for the tutor's benefit. You need to be clear on the objectives of classes within each course and active in using the classes effectively in your studies.

As Quantitative Methods is largely a numerical subject, classes will tend to be a combination of lecture-style explanation or introduction to a topic plus some practical demonstration of how the particular technique should be applied. In some cases this may include the opportunity for students to tackle a problem themselves and get some feedback or assistance from the tutor during the class (similar to a tutorial). The notes you make and the part you the student might play in the class will inevitably vary depending on which of the two approaches is being emphasised.

For example, a class on linear programming might start with one hour covering:

- the history of the technique, who invented it, where it was first applied, etc;
- the main assumptions behind the technique;
- steps involved in applying the technique;
- limitations of the technique.

The first of these (history) may not be very important, but at least reminds you that many of these techniques arose out of specific needs. It can sometimes be helpful as well to see that mathematical techniques do not just appear but are developed by real people!

The second topic (assumptions) can be very important if you wish to take the subject to higher levels than first year of a degree. It can also help you understand what the technique can and cannot be applied to. Most importantly, this is the kind of area that is often tested via a short question in an examination.

The third of these topics (steps) is crucial. This might just be outlined here, but will need to be reinforced by working through full examples. Getting the overall picture first can help greatly in learning how the techniques should be applied.

The fourth topic (limitations) has similar relevance to assumptions, being important for later studies and as a potential part of an exam question.

This could then be followed by another hour in which the tutor works through a linear programming problem, showing how the steps already outlined are applied in this particular context. This may be done by prepared slides, whiteboard, handout, etc.

In each of these parts of the class, the introductory explanation and the practical application of the technique, the tutor is leading the process. But you can be active at each stage also, and this can make a significant difference to the amount you actually learn. For example, during the first stage you can:

- take notes – not simply writing down what is said or copying what is on the board/slide, but actively creating your own summaries using your own words;
- ask questions – for clarification;
- take part in discussions;
- offer suggestions or give examples when the tutor looks for contributions from the class.

Crucial tip	Remember, most tutors actually welcome contributions from a class (so long as they are positive and helpful!), and an interactive context is much more conducive to learning than a one-way, dictation style.

During the second phase of numerical work you can also play an active part. This might include:

- cooperating with the tutor when contributions are asked for – e.g. if the tutor asks 'what do you think should be the next step?'
- asking the tutor to slow down or repeat a stage if you are having difficulty;
- summarising what you think has been done to get the tutor to confirm that you are on the right track;
- doing the calculations along with the tutor, rather than just writing down the results – this can also help the tutor as arithmetic mistakes are sometimes made!

Crucial tip	Modern computing, copying and communication tools make handouts and other types of material easy to produce and disseminate. But there is a danger in assuming that these can replace active learning. Even if your tutor issues handouts and model answers, you should still make the effort to produce your own notes and create your own answers during classes.

Section 2   Using textbooks and libraries

The amount of time you spend in the library looking for suitable Quantitative Methods textbooks will depend on the level at which you are studying and how central this subject is in your course. For a student, say, studying first year business studies at a university, Quantitative Methods will be one subject from perhaps eight in total. One central course text will be recommended, and for some students that will be the only text they refer to. Here are some reasons why other texts might be necessary:

- Although there are many university level textbooks on Quantitative Methods, none have been written for one specific course and so there is not going to be an exact fit between the text and your needs.
- This is a technical and diverse subject. Some topics might be explained to your satisfaction, but in other cases you might need a different approach to grasp the topic properly.
- The textbook might go into more depth than you need, and a simpler explanation might be helpful as an introduction to a topic.
- Not all textbooks have sufficient practice examples of the right standard.
- If you are required to carry out some detailed work as part of your assessed coursework, further reading beyond the main textbook might be necessary.
- You might even find that a particular topic was so interesting you decide to find out more about it!

There are many different Quantitative Methods textbooks recommended for use in degree courses.

Some of the more popular ones are:

Curwin, J. and Slater, R. (2002) *Quantitative Methods for Business Decisions*, 5th edn. Thomson Learning.
Drury, C. (2000) *Management and Cost Accounting*, 5th edn. Chapman & Hall.
Lewis, J.P. and Trail, A. (1999) *Statistics Explained*, Addison-Wesley.
Lucey, T. (1996) *Quantitative Techniques*, 5th edn. Letts Educational.
Mendenhall, W., Reinmuth, J.E. and Beaver, R.J. (1993) *Statistics for Management and Economics*. Duxbury Press.
Philips, J.L. Jr (1999) *How to Think about Statistics*, W.H. Freeman.

It is important to have your own copy of your course textbook, and this should really be the most recent edition. If this is the reference your tutor is using, then there should be a reasonable consistency between the teaching and the text in terms of structure of formulae, use of terminology, etc. It may also be the basis of some classwork or homework, and even having an older edition may not suffice as things like examples and page references will be different. In addition to the main textbook, it can be helpful to use one or two other texts as introductory material for some topics. Publications with 'Introduction to…', '…Made Simple', etc. in the titles can be a good source of easily understood explanations of Quantitative Methods or Statistics. One such example is:

Graham, A. (1999) *Teach Yourself Statistics*, 2nd edn. Hodder & Stoughton.

> Crucial tip
> Always be aware, if you are using texts other than the standard textbooks recommended by your course, that there is always some potential for confusion because terminology and formulae can vary.

One type of publication to avoid unless you take this subject to a higher level is the text aimed at the mathematics specialist. These are likely to assume knowledge that more basic texts will actually explain. The majority of their content may also be outside the scope of your course, and it can be difficult and time consuming to distinguish between the two. There are some standard ways of distinguishing between texts that would be suitable and those that would probably not be:

- **Table of contents** – does it look similar to the list in your syllabus? If it focuses entirely on one topic, it is probably too detailed and difficult.

- **Who is it aimed at** – the back cover will often state the target audience, e.g. 'For under-graduate and professional students'.

- **Read one or two pages** – did you understand them? Even flicking through the text to get a feel for its style can be informative; for example, if some pages consist entirely of formulae, it might not be a good starting point for your studies.

- **Practice examples** – these often indicate the source or level. Part way through your course you may be able to identify whether the level of examples is close to what you are expected to achieve.

- **Layout of text** – does it seem helpful? A text that has illustrations, step-by-step guides, case studies, etc. suggests it is aimed at helping the reader through the material, and this may be more suited to your needs as a 'non-specialist' than a text that looks heavy and dense in its style.

Section 3 Passing a Quantitative Methods examination

As with studying techniques, there are some standard examination techniques that more or less apply to all examinations. Your college or university should have resources that can help in this area, both in terms of materials and assistance from staff. You should make sure that by the time it comes to tackling your end of course examinations you have developed suitable techniques in the following areas:

- **Time management** – knowing how to allocate time to individual questions or parts of questions in order to maximise your chances of passing the examination.

- **Question spotting** – a dangerous approach is to narrow your study or revision to the minimum number of topics, leaving yourself exposed to the possibility of not being able to tackle the required number of questions in the examination.

- **Presentation of answers** – you should know what the required formats or layouts are for each kind of question.

- **Writing style** – Quantitative Methods examinations can include some narrative questions, so you need to be able to write clearly and concisely to score marks quickly.

- **Writing** – nerves and time constraint can lead to poor handwriting, so you should take care to write legibly.

> Crucial tip   'If I cannot read it, I cannot mark it' – favourite quote from examiners!

Most tutors will hopefully give you suitable practice during the course to prepare you for the actual examination. It is essential that you take these seriously throughout your studies if you want to give yourself a good chance of passing. The main vehicles for providing this practice will be the following:

- **Examples during class time** – led by the tutor or done by you with some review by the tutor.

- **Mock examinations** – often provided near the end of a course as a means of assessing students without the marks counting towards your final result. This is probably the most important means of developing good examination technique, so you should prepare for them and attempt them as though they were the real thing. You should also take careful note of comments made by the tutor once you get your marked script back.
- **Homework, coursework, past papers and practice questions in textbooks** – all these should be used to practise each topic on the syllabus until you feel able to tackle examination questions in the required time.

In addition to these general issues, there are some things that apply to Quantitative Methods examinations that are not found in all other degree subjects. One is the practice of issuing a formula sheet with the examination paper and a set of statistical tables. As you work through this study guide you will find reference to various formulae and tables in connection with specific topics. Some course organisers take the view that the test in the examination is not whether you know the formula by heart, but whether you can apply it properly, and so the main formulae are provided in the examination. As you use this guide and other materials such as textbooks, you will find that the same formula can appear in slightly different forms or use different symbols. This is a potential area for confusion, so you must check with your course tutor which formulae will appear on the sheet provided in the examination and what form these will take. The same applies to statistical tables – find out what is provided so that you can become familiar with the formats used.

> Crucial tip Different examinations emphasise different skills – memorising, interpreting, applying a mechanical process, etc. You need to understand what the emphasis is on in the examinations that you are attempting so that you can gear your study, revision and examination technique towards that.

Another simple issue, but nonetheless and important one, is the choice and use of a calculator. This will be an essential tool in your examination, so you need to be comfortable with how it works and what it is capable of. Before choosing one, you should check with your tutor what types of calculator are not allowed in the examination itself (usually programmable calculators are banned). And you should also seek advice on what additional functions would be useful. Beyond the very basic calculator that has $0 - 9$, $+$, $-$, x, $/$, $=$, $\%$ there are others that have mathematical, statistical, financial or scientific functions, some of which can save time in an examination. As a minimum, you should have a good memory function (perhaps more than one), $\sqrt{}$ (square root), x^2 (square) and $x!$ (factorial), and then you should take advice about other functions that would be helpful for your particular course. Avoid, however, going for the most expensive calculator with the most buttons on it – it is only of use as a tool if it is relevant to your needs and you know how to use it!

You will find a number of Crucial Tips throughout this study guide that give advice on exam technique and presentation of answers. Here are some final points of a general nature, however.

Numerical questions:

- Use standard formats where appropriate.
- Don't cram figures and formulae into small spaces – spread them out on the page so that it is easier for the examiner to follow and make notes.

- Show all your workings – even if you used a calculator, you should show the steps you have gone through to get to a result.

- Cross reference your workings to the relevant part of the answer if necessary.

- If you realise you made a numerical error near the beginning of an answer, it is not usually worth going back and reworking the whole answer again – the time can be better used elsewhere.

- Check answers for 'reasonableness'. If you find your answer says the average wage for a group of people is £500,000 then you presumably made a mistake somewhere!

Narrative questions:

- Note the number of marks available and tailor your answer accordingly.

- Be concise and precise. Marks are usually given for separate points, so saying the same thing four times will get you one mark, not four.

- Try and show understanding as well as a good memory. For example, if asked to explain the difference between mean, mode and median, as well as giving textbook definitions you could give an example of each.

- Attempt them! As Quantitative Methods is largely seen as a numerical subject, there is a temptation to focus all effort on numerical parts of the exam. Even if narrative sections are only worth four or five marks each, this can still amount to as much as 25% of the entire examination marks, so doing these well can seriously improve your chances of passing.

> Crucial tip Marks can often be scored very quickly if narrative questions are tackled effectively, so it is worth preparing for them and allocating time to them in the examination.

The examination at the end of the course is viewed by most students as the focal point of the process, and everything else (classes, textbooks, homework, etc.) leads up to it. Passing the examination is one indication that the course has been successful. Other indicators such as being able to apply some of the techniques in later life might not seem so important at this stage. Because of its importance, it makes sense that you are familiar with all its requirements. So as well as making preparations in terms of study, revision, practice, etc., you need to know what will be expected of you at the examination itself. Some of the following will seem obvious or common sense, but it is still worth reinforcing the point that you must know the answers to all these questions well in advance of the examination:

- How long is the exam?

- How many sections are in the paper and how many questions are in each section?

- What freedom of choice do I have in which questions to answer?

- Are all questions worth the same number of marks?

- Which of the following are provided: formula sheet, statistical tables, graph paper, financial analysis paper?

- What types of calculator are allowed?

- What size of desk is provided?

- Where does the examination take place?

- Who sets the paper – internal or external?
- Who assesses my script?
- What are the arrangements for appeals or resitting?
- Does coursework count towards the final mark? If so, what is the proportion?
- Can I compensate for a poor result in one subject with a good pass in another?
- What is the pass mark?

As you go through the course, you will probably find that there are many other questions that could be added to this list.

Crucial tip	Know your enemy! Examinations are potentially nerve-wracking affairs, but this can be minimised by being familiar with the arrangements. You should not know what the questions will be in the examination paper, but you should not be surprised by any of the format and other arrangements. This can make a big difference in keeping your anxiety to a manageable level.

INTRODUCTION TO QUANTITATIVE METHODS

Chapter summary

The title of this textbook is Quantitative Methods, but you will find that the material covered here can appear under several different headings, e.g. quantitative techniques, operational research, analytical techniques, business mathematics, mathematical models, etc. The term 'statistics' is also used, sometimes on its own, but often in conjunction with one of the other terms just mentioned. This text uses the term quantitative methods to refer to the broad range of techniques that are covered. Many of the techniques are related, and each chapter has a list of relevant links where appropriate. Not every technique that could be included under quantitative methods is given attention here, as the emphasis is on covering the most important techniques in a thorough but user-friendly manner.

In this chapter we will look at some of the fundamental concepts in quantitative methods. These are all important for understanding later topics.

Studying this chapter will help you to:

- understand why quantitative methods are useful;
- produce and interpret frequency distributions;
- calculate and distinguish between the mean, mode and median;
- understand and calculate standard deviations and variances;
- understand the different forms of skewness.

Assessment targets

Target 1

You may be required to arrange data into more meaningful formats, such as tables and charts, and then use these to interpret the information. Question 1 at the end of this chapter tests your ability to do this.

Target 2

The mean, mode and median are types of average that you might be asked to calculate and distinguish. The mean in particular can be incorporated with other techniques that are covered in later chapters. Question 2 at the end of this chapter tests you on calculating each of these averages.

Target 3

The standard deviation is another fundamental topic that is widely used in quantitative methods. Question 3 at the end of this chapter tests that you can calculate the standard deviation of a set of values.

Crucial concepts

These are the key terms and concepts you will meet in this chapter:

Class interval	Mode
Cumulative frequency distribution	Normal distribution
Dispersion	Range
Frequency distribution	Skewness
Grouped data	Standard deviation
Mean	Ungrouped data
Median	Variance

Relevant links

As these topics are fundamental, their relevance applies to all the techniques discussed in the following chapters. Obviously, they are not all equally relevant to every chapter, so the key links are highlighted at the beginning of each of the chapters.

Section 1 — Why quantitative methods and statistics are useful

What are you studying?

In this section we will look the ways in which quantitative methods and statistics can be helpful as we try and understand numerical data, make decisions, present information in a meaningful way, etc.

How will you be assessed on this?

Understanding the need for these techniques is important if you are to be able to apply the techniques in the correct context, understand how the result should be interpreted, make the right decisions in applying the results, etc. Examiners like to test this ability by adding sections on to numerical questions that focus on interpretation, explanation and application. So it is important to be able to write coherently about techniques, as well as working through the calculations.

Quantitative methods are useful in helping decision-makers, whether they are managers, politicians, coaches, investors, etc. In the course of taking a decision, it is usually necessary to do three things with the available data:

- Describe the data in a meaningful way.
- Examine the data to find out what relevant information can be taken from it.
- Use that information to make predictions or estimates about it.

Sometimes decisions can be taken without recourse to detailed and systematic analysis of the data. A businessman may simply 'feel' that now is the right time to launch a new venture. A football manager may have a 'hunch' that a young player is worth buying. A doctor may through experience judge that a particular drug is more effective than another alternative. However, it is becoming more and more the case (although that is perhaps a 'hunch' on my part!) that in all walks of life people are looking for something more tangible to base decisions on. This may be partly out of a desire for making better decisions, and partly out of a need to defend or justify decisions.

In the examples given, the decisions might be different if the businessman was given information on the percentage of new ventures that are successful at this stage in an economic cycle. The football manager might think twice if told that the player was 5 inches smaller than the average international footballer. And the doctor may revise their opinion if presented with figures detailing the recovery time for groups of patients taking the two drugs. So, to make well-informed decisions, we need to have the right data in an understandable form in the first place; we need to know how to analyse it so that we know what it can tell us; and we need to use that information in coming to a decision.

Section 2   Presenting data

What are you studying?

In this section we will look at different ways of summarising data and presenting it in meaningful ways.

How will you be assessed on this?

This is the first thing you have to do in many assessments. A problem may be presented to you containing a mass of data. In order to analyse this and come to a conclusion, you first need to organise the data in a suitable format, such as an ordered table or a graph. Being able to do this accurately, and also quickly, is an important aspect of examination technique.

If a sample of data is gathered over a period of time, the results might initially seem meaningless (note – sampling is discussed in more detail in Chapter 4). So a first step will be to decide how to make this more understandable. For example, if you observe waiting times at a dentist's surgery, for 20 patients the results (in minutes) might look like this:

7	5	18	1
1	6	4	4
8	7	10	18
2	5	3	4
4	9	12	2

Without summarising or ordering the data some basic comments could be made about the figures. For example, the sample suggests that the maximum waiting time is 18 minutes, and that most patients wait less than 10 minutes. We could make it a bit more detailed by counting the number that wait less than 10 minutes, i.e. 16 out of 20, or 80%. This gives a more specific result, and this figure can then perhaps be used for other purposes (such as deciding how many chairs need to be provided to cater for all waiting patients). Before making such analysis, however, it can be helpful to present the information in a more useful manner to save us doing things like counting up all the items that meet particular criteria.

One obvious step is to list the items in order:

1	1	2	2
3	4	4	4
4	5	5	6
7	7	8	9
10	12	18	18

This makes it easier to pick out the highest number, showing the longest waiting time. It is also easier to see the proportion that is less than 10 minutes, i.e. 4 rows out of the 5, therefore 80%. But ordering information can be done in different ways, and there are choices to be made depending on the use to which the data is to be put. In a list of 20 items, showing each item as an individual piece of data in the table is acceptable because the list is small enough for the user to be able to handle it. If there were 500 items, this would be much more difficult. So another way of making the data easier to interpret is by grouping it.

Crucial concepts **Grouped** data results from recording values and grouping them into classes, showing the frequency for each class. Raw data, where all items are listed without being grouped, is **ungrouped data.**

Where data has been grouped into classes, the range of values covered by each class is the **class interval.** The class intervals should be of equal size to allow easier analysis of tables and charts containing grouped data.

The decision as to how to group data is sometimes purely subjective, but in some cases there might be an 'obvious' approach. Likewise, some groupings seem natural (such as placing items into class intervals of 0–9, 10–19, etc.) while others would seem unnatural (such as grouping 0–13, 14–27, etc.). In the example above, the waiting times ranges from 1 minute to 18 minutes and there are 20 observations in total. We can use this information to select a grouping approach that makes sense. Grouping into 0–9 and 10–19, would only give us two classes, and this would not be particularly helpful. Grouping into 0–1, 2–3, etc. would give us too many classes. A balance between having a reasonable number of classes without the range of each class interval being too large would be to have, say, four or five classes, as follows:

Group	Frequency
0–4	9
5–9	7
10–14	2
15–19	2

This analysis gives us a slightly different 'picture' of the data. It is now clearer that most of the waiting times are towards the bottom end of the range. Another way that is often used in everyday situations is to refer to the 'average'. We will look at different types of average in more detail in the next section, but it is worth noting that using the two sets of data in this example (i.e. grouped and ungrouped), we can calculate two different figures for the most commonly used average, ie the mean.

> **Crucial concept** The **mean** is found by adding together all the values in a set of data and dividing this figure by the number of values.

From the ungrouped data, the mean is calculated as:

$$\frac{130}{20} = 6.5 \, minutes$$

Using the grouped data, we need to calculate a value for each group. This is normally done by selecting the mid-point in the range of values for each group and multiplying by the number of items (frequency).

Group	Mid-value x	Frequency f	fx
0–4	2	9	18
5–9	7	7	49
10–14	12	2	24
15–19	17	2	34

So, the mean of the waiting times based on grouped data is:

$$\frac{125}{20} = 6.25 \, minutes$$

> **Crucial tip** The difference in means between grouped and ungrouped data arises because when data items are grouped together, some of the accuracy is lost, i.e. all items in a group are assumed to be equal to the mid-value of the group.

As long as the grouping is done in a reasonable way, and groups are not too large or small, the slight loss of accuracy can be accepted as there is an increase in the ease with which the

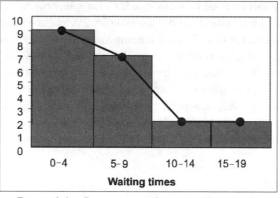

Figure 1.1   Presenting information in a graph

data can be analysed. This can be seen when it comes to presenting information in a graph as in Figure 1.1.

It is clear from the graph in Figure 1.1 that the waiting times are heavily weighted to the lower values. This is the grouped frequency distribution of the waiting times. A frequency distribution for the ungrouped data would have a similar shape, but the line would be smoother as it would be linked to all data items instead of just four as in the grouped version.

Crucial concept   A **frequency distribution** shows the variable values and the number of occurrences of each value. In the case of a **grouped frequency distribution**, the number of occurrences of each group of values is shown.

Another way of presenting the same data is first of all to calculate cumulative figures, i.e. instead of showing the values **within** each class, the table (and associated chart shown in Figure 1.2) shows frequencies **up to** the upper limit of each class interval.

Group	Mid-value x	Frequency f		fx
0–4	2	9	9	18
5–9	7	7	16	49
10–14	12	2	18	24
15–19	17	2	20	34

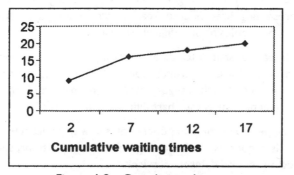

Figure 1.2   Cumulative chart

The chart in Figure 1.2 can be used to work out, for example, how many waiting times were 6 minutes or less. The value 6 minutes is within the class 5 to 9, represented here by the mid-point of 7. The points on the line for class 2 and 7 (i.e. the known points below and above 6) can be read off against the y-axis (i.e. the vertical axis on the left) as 9 and 16, so the number of waiting times equal to or below 6 minutes must be somewhere in this range. As the chart just has a straight line between these two points, we cannot be certain what the true figure is, but the chart would suggest the answer is 12.5, i.e. approximately 12 or 13. Going back to the original data, we find that the true figure is actually 12. Clearly, this would have been easier to read from the chart if all 20 values were plotted, rather than just the class mid-points. This is shown in the chart in Figure 1.3.

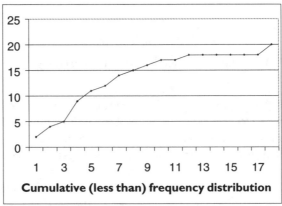

Figure 1.3   Plot of all points

You may have noticed how several different types of chart have been used so far in this chapter. This is a topic in itself, but we will not look in depth here at the merits of all the different types and how they should be used, but it is useful to consider some of the basic dos and don'ts here.

Histograms	The chart for grouped data in Figure 1.1 shows a bar for each class. These bars have no gaps in between as the series is continuous.
Bar charts	Separate categories are indicated by non-adjacent bars in the chart. Useful for getting an instant picture of the relative sizes of different categories. May be shown vertically or horizontally. All bars in the chart should be drawn with the same width. Interpreting the chart can also be helped by arranging the bars in a sensible order.
Compound bar charts	Bars are grouped together, e.g. each category may have three bars, representing three different year's figures. Having too many together can make the chart confusing and difficult to read.
Component bar charts	Each bar is split into different components (e.g. vertical bar split into horizontal 'slices'). Useful for sub-cateogries, such as showing the proportions of each category made up of males and females. Again, too many components makes the chart difficult to interpret.
Pie charts	This type shows the component parts of a single item (like the slices of a pie). This is a good way of showing relative proportions, such as amounts of a budget spent on different services.

Pictograms These use symbols or pictures to represent items, such as matchstick people to represent individuals (or some multiple such as 1,000 people). These are useful for giving a less abstract respresentation of the data.

Scattergraphs Sets of paired data are plotted on the graph, with the two axes representing the two features being compared. Useful for showing trends and relationships between pairs, such as number of pupils and number of teachers.

Quick test

1. Explain the difference between a frequency distribution and a cumulative frequency distribution.

2 What kind of chart would you use to represent the amounts a student spends on food, rent, books, travel and entertainment?

Section 3	Averages – mean, mode and median

What are you studying?
The concept of averages is a common one, and you are probably used to using the term. In quantitative methods there is more than one kind of average, and it is necessary to be able to distinguish between them and calculate the different values.

How will you be assessed on this?
This is not a topic than normally appears in isolation. It is, however, a key area, and is essential for many of the other topics being covered in this textbook. The most common average is the mean, and several statistical techniques require use of the mean in formulae. The other two, the mode and the median, are not so central, but you may be required to calculate them and explain the pros and cons of each type of average.

The common feature the three averages have is that they all reduce a set of data to a single figure, and this figure is in some way seen as central, representative or typical of the set as a whole. So rather than being simply presented with a list of what 100 people earn in a month, a single figure can be drawn from this set and presented as 'average earnings'. Take, for example, the following monthly earnings for a salesperson over the course of a year. Let's assume that she is being paid on a commission only basis:

	Earnings £
January	2,100
February	2,100
March	2,100
April	1,900
May	2,000
June	4,200
July	2,400
August	1,800
September	2,100
October	1,000
November	1,900
December	1,000

The mean (or arithmetic mean) is usually denoted by $\bar{x}$ (called 'x bar'), and for this data set is found using the following formula:

$$\text{Mean} = \frac{\Sigma x}{n} = \frac{24,600}{12} = 2,050$$

The top part of the formula (numerator) simply means 'all the values of x added together', and the bottom part (denominator) is the number of values of x. The expression Σx is referred to as 'sigma x'.

There are several advantages to using this figure. In particular, the mean includes the values of all items in the set, i.e. if we changed any one of the monthly earnings, the mean would change as well. It is also well understood, even by people without a mathematical background. One disadvantage is that the value of £2,050 does not appear on the list of earnings for the year; the closest are £2,000 and £2,100. A further criticism of it might be that including all values might mean that it is distorted by the existence of extreme values. In this example the months of December (perhaps nobody wants to buy the product over the festive period) and October when she is on holiday do not reflect normal activity. And perhaps the success in June is a one-off and also not representative. These criticisms are perhaps more to do with the selection of a sample than a criticism of the mean itself as a calculation of the average. If individual values are deemed to be extreme and likely to distort the mean, then it is legitimate to exclude them from the calculation.

> Crucial concept The **mean** is the average value found by adding all values in a set together and dividing by the number of values.

One of the criticisms of the mean was that it can result in a figure that does not actually appear in the data set, as in the above example. The next approach to finding an average, the mode, does not have that drawback. The mode is found by arranging the data to identify the number of times each value appears. The mode is the one that occurs the most often. In our example, this would be £2,100, as it occurs four times during the year:

Earnings £	Frequency
1,000	2
1,800	1
1,900	2
2,000	1
2,100	4
2,400	1
4,200	1

This figure can be useful when there is some tendency to cluster at one representative value. In some instances, however, it may be necessary to group items together or round the figures to the nearest, say, 10 or 100 to avoid having a list in which every value appears only once. It may also be the case that the mode is near one end of the range of values, undermining the sense of the figure being representative.

> Crucial concept The **mode** is the value that occurs most often in a data set.

The third approach is to calculate the median. This is simply the middle value in the set of data. If, for example, there are five items in a set, the median will be the third one after they have being placed in order of size. In the earnings example there is an even number of items, and this means we must calculate the mean of the two middle items:

Earnings £

1,000
1,000
1,800
1,900
1,900
2,000 ⎫ **middle values**
2,100 ⎭
2,100
2,100
2,400
4,200

The median, then, is the mean of £2,000 and £2,100, which is £2,050. Coincidentally this is the same as the mean, but that is not always the case.

> Crucial concept   The **median** in a set of data with an odd number of items is the value of the middle item when they are arranged in order of size.

An advantage of the median is that it will always have an equal number of values above and below it in the set of data. But it is still important to check that the figure obtained is realistic or sensible before using it for further analysis. For example, the following table shows goals scored for two football teams, and both have the same median, but it would be misleading to use this as an assessment of the relative performance of the two teams which are clearly very different:

Team A	Team B
0	0
0	1
0	1
2	2
2	2
2	4
2	4

The median in each case is 2 goals, but Team A have scored a total of 8 goals compared with 14 for Team B.

Quick test

What would be the most useful average to calculate for the results of a class of students in a single examination?

Section 4 Dispersion, standard deviation and the normal distribution

What are you studying?

In this section we will look at different ways of assessing the variation in a set of values. We will be introducing some very important concepts that will be essential for later chapters.

How will you be assessed on this?

Being able to describe the dispersion of a set of values, calculate and use standard deviation, and apply the normal distribution are all necessary for techniques we will be considering in more detail later. For example, sampling and hypothesis testing are covered in Chapters 4 and 5, and examination questions on these topics will require an ability to apply the skills we are going to look at in this section.

When we consider a set of data, one issue is the extent to which the values are dispersed. For example, are they all close together or do they cover a wide range? Are there more at the top end of the range, in the middle or at the bottom end? Two ways of getting information to answer these, and other, questions are to draw the 'shape' of the distribution and to calculate statistics that measure features of this distribution. A key aspect of this topic is the concept of the normal distribution.

> Crucial tip   The normal distribution is fundamental to later chapters on statistical in-
> ference and hypothesis testing. Understanding the main features of the
> normal distribution at this stage will save you a lot of grief later on in
> your studies!

> Crucial concept   The **normal distribution** is a model of the distribution of continuous
> variables. It is symmetrical and 'bell-shaped' with infinite 'tails'. The mean,
> mode and median are equal.

The normal distribution can be seen in a large number of natural occurrences, such as height of men or women, the expected life of a batch of batteries, etc. For example, the chart in Figure 1.4 shows the results of testing 150 batches of self-assembly furniture packs (100 packs per batch) to check that the dimensions meet standard specifications. The figures represent the number of errors per batch.

Your first reaction might be to point out that the chart is neither symmetrical nor bell-shaped! But that is not really the point. The definition above referred to the normal distribution being a 'model' of the distribution of continuous variables. In other words, the number of packs with errors per 100 has an underlying normal distribution, but not every sample taken will have a perfect bell-shaped and symmetrical curve. If the tests were taken an infinite number of times, we would expect the results to follow the normal curve, but a series of 150 is not large enough to replicate that theoretical result.

The chart clearly shows that there is some variation in the results for different batches. One measure of this variation is the overall range of results, which is from 1 at the lower end to 11 at the top end, giving a range of 10 errors per hundred.

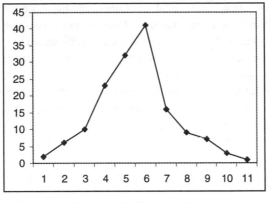

Figure 1.4   Test results

> **Crucial concept**   The **range** is the difference between the upper extreme value and the lower extreme value.

This information can be used along with calculation of the mean, mode and median to give a better understanding of the results. As a measure, however, this is imperfect because it is directly affected by any unusually large or small values (a similar criticism was made of the median). What we know so far is that the values range from 1 to 11, and we can easily calculate the mean, which is approximately 5.5. What would be useful to know in addition to this is the **extent** to which the results vary from this mean of 5.5. This is known as dispersion, and we will look at the two principal measures of dispersion here.

> **Crucial concept**   **Dispersion** is the variation in a set of values, and is measured by the standard deviation and the variance.

The two measures of dispersion, variance and standard deviation, are closely linked. This is clear from the two formulae used to calculate them:

$$\text{Standard deviation} \quad \sigma = \sqrt{\frac{\Sigma(x-\mu)^2}{N}}$$

$$\text{Variance} \quad \sigma = \frac{\Sigma(x-\mu)^2}{N}$$

(Note: these formula need to be adjusted for grouped data.)

where $(x - \mu)$ = the difference between the mean and each value in the data set, and N is the number of items.

> **Crucial concept**   The **standard deviation** is the most important measure of dispersion. Like the **variance**, it is based on a comparison of each value and the arithmetic mean. The standard deviation is the square root of the variance.

These can be calculated using a statistical calculator or the STDEVP function in the Excel spreadsheet program. If there is a large number of items, the process can be quite laborious; for example, the standard deviation for the above example is 1.85 errors per 100 packs, but as there are 150 values to consider, this takes a few minutes, even using a spreadsheet.

> **Crucial tip** A lot of examination questions will provide the standard deviation figure for you, so you should concentrate on being able to use it in other processes and understand what it means.

Example

What is the standard deviation of the length in pages of following set of student assignments:

5, 4, 7, 6, 6, 10, 4

x	x-μ	(x-μ)²
5	−1	1
4	−2	4
7	1	1
6	0	0
6	0	0
10	4	16
4	−2	4
Σx = 42		Σ(x-μ)² = 26

Mean = 42/7 = 6 pages

Variance = 26/7 = 3.71 pages

Standard deviation = $\sqrt{3.71} = 1.93$ pages

> **Crucial tip** These formula hold true where all relevant details about a population are known. If you are dealing with a sample, the formulae need to be modified, and this is shown in more detail in Chapter 4.

One further term you should know is 'skewness'. This refers to the extent to which the shape of the distribution is symmetrical. We have already seen that the normal distribution is symmetrical, therefore no skewness exists. Other distributions may be positively or negatively skewed, as shown in Figures 1.5 and 1.6.

> **Crucial concept** **Skewness** refers to a lack of symmetry in a distribution. A positively skewed distribution has a peak towards the left (i.e. lower values), and a negatively skewed distribtion has a peak towards the right of the distribution.

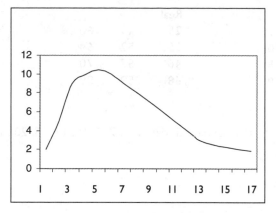

Figure 1.5   Positive skewness

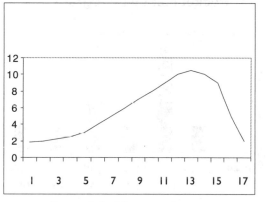

Figure 1.6   Negative skewness

Quick test

1. What are the two main measures of dispersion?
2. What are the main characteristics of the normal distribution?

Crucial examples

1. The following data relates to daily pocket money (in pence) received by a group of 12 year olds:

100	100
300	75
100	150
200	200
250	125

   Use the data to produce a histogram and a cumulative frequency chart.
2. Calculate the mean, mode and median of the following results (out of 100) for a class of students sitting a mock test and then the real examination, and comment on the usefulness of the results:

Mock			Real		
18	42	49	25	49	60
25	45	50	35	52	64
28	46	65	46	57	70
35	46	80	48	59	80

3. Calculate the variance and standard deviation of 7, 9, 10, 12, 15, 20 metres.

Answers

1. See Figures 1.7 and 1.8.

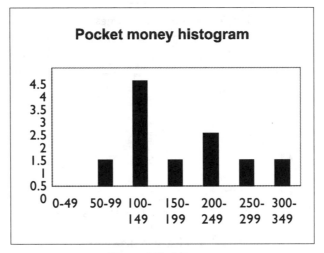

Figure 1.7   Histogram

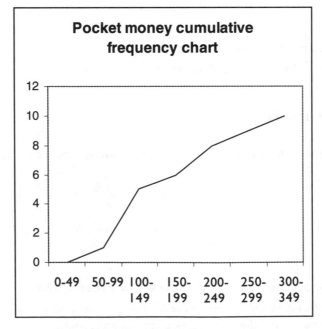

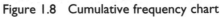

Figure 1.8   Cumulative frequency chart

2.

	Mock	Real
Mean	44.1	53.8
Mode	46	35
Median	45.5	54.5

Comments:

- Mean and median have increased, reflecting overall improvement in performance.
- Mode, however, is lower, but this is clearly misleading.
- Different picture could be obtained by grouping the data, e.g. into class intervals of 10 marks – mode (i.e. modal class) would then be 40–49 for mock, and equally 40–49 and 50–59 for real examination.

3. Mean   = 12.17
   N   = 6
   $\Sigma(x-\mu)^2$ = 110.83
   Variance   = 110.83/6 = 18.47 metres
   Std dev   = $\sqrt{18.47}$ = 4.30 metres

Crucial reading and research

Reading

Curwin, J. and Slater, R. (2002) *Quantitative Methods for Business Decisions*, 5th edn. Thomson Learning. See Chapter 5: Measures of Location (pp. 103–17), Chapter 6: Measures of Dispersion (pp. 123–38) and Chapter 10: The Normal Distribution (pp. 220–34).

Lucey, T. (1996) *Quantitative Techniques*, 5th edn. Letts Educational. See Chapter 4: Statistics – Introduction (pp. 45–55).

Research

Spreadsheet packages like Microsoft Excel provide useful facilities that can help you with the topics discussed in this chapter. Some of the calculations shown as formulae in the chapter can be performed quickly using the functions contained in Excel; for example, the STDEVP is one of the statistical functions. It is worth browsing the range of functions (found in the Insert, Functions menu) or using the Help facility to see what the spreadsheet can do to support your studies in this and the other chapters in this book.

You could also look further into the range of presentation types that are in common use today. Analysing textbooks, newspapers, magazines, etc. can give you examples of charts, diagrams and tables that present data in different ways for different effects. Again, Excel has a range of chart options that are very simple to use.

CHAPTER 2

PROBABILITY

Chapter summary

This chapter introduces the topic of probability, which is an important topic in its own right and is also necessary for use in other techniques.

Studying this chapter will help you to:

- understand and use the addition and multiplication rules of probability;
- use the rules of probability to calculate the probability of certain events;
- distinguish between dependent and independent events;
- distinguish between combinations and permutations;
- understand the principles of conditional probability and Bayes' rule;
- use Venn diagrams in calculating probabilities.

Assessment targets

Target 1

In your assessment you may be asked to calculate the probability of an event occurring given a certain set of circumstances. This frequently appears in examinations with a multiple-choice element. Question 1 at the end of the chapter assesses your ability to calculate basic probabilities using the addition and multiplication rules.

Target 2

You may be given a situation where the conditional rule needs to be employed to calculate the probability of an event. Question 2 at the end of the chapter tests your ability to calculate probabilities using the conditional rule.

Target 3

Some situations require the calculation of the probability of an event not occurring. Question 3 at the end of the chapter tests the requirement to calculate complementary probabilities.

Target 4

It is important to be able to identify where particular distributions should be applied and use the available data to determine probabilities for certain outcomes. Question 4 at the end of this chapter provides some practice in calculating probabilities for normal and binomial distributions.

Crucial concepts

These are the key terms and concepts you will meet in this chapter:

Addition rule	Independent event
Bayes' rule	Multiplication rule
Binomial distribution	Mutually exclusive events
Combinations	Permutations
Complementary probability	Probability
Conditional event	Probability distribution
Conditional rule	Sample space
Continuous distribution	Uncertainty
Dependent event	Venn diagrams
Discrete distribution	

Relevant links

Basic probability rules are used in many of the techniques outlined in this text. In particular, **Chapter 3** uses probability in the context of decision trees and other decision-making techniques. The discussion in Section 5 on probability distributions continues from **Chapter 1**, where the normal distribution was introduced. Distributions are also relevant to **Chapters 4** and **5**.

Section 1   Basic probability

What are you studying?

In this section we outline the basic concepts of probability and the main rules required for working out probabilities.

How will you be assessed on this?

Probability is an important topic that appears in various forms in different quantitative techniques and in different business situations. For example, a business may be given several alternatives and would then need to assess which is the best one to choose. While you may not be assessed directly or in depth on this content, you will certainly draw upon this knowledge when analysing business or financial decisions that involve uncertainty.

You are no doubt used to using terms like 'probability', 'likelihood', 'chance', 'risk', etc. in everyday speech when you need to express whether something might happen or not. You will also from time to time use more specific terms like '99 per cent certain' or '50–50 chance'. These terms are not meant to be precise, but give an expression of **how** likely an event or outcome is (in your opinion).

While this is perfectly acceptable in discussing situations such as who might win a sporting competition, when it comes to business decisions there is often a need for a more precise or reliable way of expressing this uncertainty so that managers can be assisted in making decisions. Probability, as outlined in this chapter, can be thought of as the quantification of that uncertainty.

Crucial concept	**Probability** is the proportion of times that a particular event is likely to occur in a large number of trials for that event.

The result can be expressed as a decimal fraction (e.g. 0.5), as a proportion (e.g. $\frac{1}{2}$) or as a percentage (e.g. 50%). It is important to understand what these results actually mean, and using some simple examples to learn the basics will stand you in good stead when it comes to more complex situations. The standard scenarios used for demonstrating simple probability are tossing a coin, throwing a die and selecting a playing card from a pack.

In order to work out probabilities for different situations you will need to use various rules. These are expressed using standard abbreviations and notation. The definition of probability can therefore be expressed as:

$$P(E) = \frac{\text{Number of favourable outcomes}}{\text{Total number of possible outcomes}}$$

where P(E) is the probability of a particular event occurring. For example, if a coin is tossed, what is the probability of 'heads'?

$$P(\text{heads}) = \frac{\text{Heads}}{\text{Heads or tails}} = \frac{1}{2} \text{ or } 0.5$$

Crucial tip	Although you could work this out without using the full expression, you should get into the habit of using this and other expressions as they will be essential in more difficult problems.

The result of a probability of 0.5 for getting 'heads' indicates that there is an equal chance of getting a favourable result ('heads') and of getting an unfavourable result ('tails' or 'not heads'). The larger the fraction, the more likely a favourable result is, and the smaller is the likelihood of a less favourable result. So a result close to 1 indicates high probability and close to zero indicates low probability. You can think of this as a scale of probability:

0		0.5		1
Impossibility	Low probability	50–50 chance	High probability	Certainty

For example, if you throw a six-sided die (assuming for now it is not biased), what is the probability of getting a result of 8, or of getting a result between 1 and 6?

$P(8) = 0$ (i.e. it is impossible because none of the sides have 8 spots)
$P(between\ 1\ and\ 6) = 1$ (i.e. it is certain because all the possible results fall into this range)

Some other important terms you need to understand and apply relate to different types of event, i.e. **mutually exclusive events, independent events** and **dependent events**.

> Crucial concept **Mutually exclusive events** are events that cannot take place at the same time. If one happens the other(s) cannot occur.

For example, in a pack of 52 cards consisting of four suits, if we select one card and it is a heart, this automatically excludes the possibility of the card being a spade. In other words, there is no overlap between the set of cards that are hearts and those that are spades.

> Crucial concepts Two or more events are **independent** if the occurrence or non-occurrence of one does not affect the occurrence or non-occurrence of any other(s). Two or more events are said to be **dependent** when the probability of the second event is conditional on the first event having taken place.

For example, if I toss a coin and the result is 'heads', this event does not affect the probability of getting 'heads' next time I toss the coin. Even if I get 'heads' four times in a row, the fifth time I toss the coin the probability of 'heads' is still 0.5 because this is **independent** of previous tosses. On the other hand, if I select a card from a pack of 52 and the card is the ace of clubs, if I don't replace this card the probability of getting a club next time is reduced as there are now only 12 clubs in the pack, not 13 (so these two events are not **independent**).

We have seen in some of these simple examples how it is possible to list all the possible outcomes of an action. This is referred to as the **sample space**, and **Venn diagrams** can be used to represent outcomes and show how they are related.

> Crucial concepts The **sample space** is a list of all possible outcomes of an event. A **Venn diagram** is a pictorial method of showing a sample space classified into different groups.

For example, a class of 20 students is made up as follows:

	Male	Female	Total
English	2	4	6
Scottish	3	1	4
Welsh	3	3	6
Irish	2	2	4
	10	10	20

If we wanted to assess the probabilities of selecting an English or male student from the class we could use a Venn diagram as in Figure 2.1.

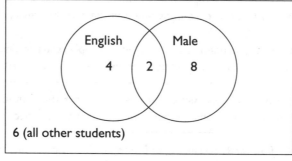

Figure 2.1   Venn diagram

The left circle represents all the English students, and the right circle all the male students. As two of the students are both English and male, the two circles overlap. We can use the diagram to calculate certain probabilities, for example:

- The probability of selecting a student from the class who is **either** male **or** English.

  P (English or male)   = All items in either circle or in both as a proportion of the total in the class

  $$= \frac{4+2+8}{20} = \frac{7}{10}$$

- The probability of selecting a student from the class who is **both** male **and** English:

  P (English and male) = All items that are in both circles

  $$= \frac{2}{20} = \frac{1}{10}$$

If you look back at the original table you should be able to see that these answers are correct.

Quick test

1. What is the difference between independent and dependent events?

2. What is a sample space?

Section 2   Rules of probability

What are you studying?
Here we look at the two fundamental rules of probability, the **addition rule** and the **multiplication rule**. Once again, these can seem obvious when considering simple examples, but it is important that you understand them and can apply them so that you are able to tackle more difficult questions.

How will you be assessed on this?
You are not likely to be assessed directly on these rules alone, but they are necessary for techniques such as expected values, decision trees and other managerial decision-making problems.

The **addition rule** is used where, rather than just wanting to know the probability of a single outcome, we want to know the probability of *either* that outcome *or* one or more alternative outcomes. This rule can first of all be used to calculate the probability of two or more **mutually exclusive events**.

Crucial concept   According to the **addition rule**, if a test has several **mutually exclusive events**, then the probability of alternative events in a single test is the sum of their individual probabilities:

P(A or B) = P(A) + P(B)
P(A or B or C) = P(A) + P(B) + P(C)

For example, the probability of either 'heads' or 'tails' is 1 (i.e. certainty) because the outcome must be one of the two. The probability of selecting either a heart or a club from a pack of cards

is:

$$\frac{13}{52} + \frac{13}{52} = \frac{26}{52} = \frac{1}{2}$$

The addition rule can also be used where events are not **mutually exclusive**, and there is an 'overlap' between the two as we saw in the Venn diagram above. As the overlap area relates to both events, we need to avoid counting it twice, so the addition rule we have just looked at needs to be amended.

Crucial concept   According to the **addition rule**, if a test has two events that are not **mutually exclusive**, then the probability of alternative events in a single test is the sum of their individual probabilities less the probability of both occurring:

P(A or B) = P(A) + P(B) − P(A and B)

For example, we might want to know the probability of throwing a die and getting an odd number or a number divisible by three:

P(odd)   = 0.5

P(divisible by 3)   = 0.333

P(odd and divisible by 3)= 0.1667

The outcomes that meet the criterion of being odd are 1, 3 and 5. The outcomes that meet the divisible by three criterion are 3 and 6. As the outcome 3 appears in both sets we would count its probability twice if we simply added these two probabilities together, so we need to deduct this overlap:

P(odd or divisible by 3) = P(odd) + P(divisible by three) − P(odd and divisible by three)

= 0.5 + 0.333 − 0.167

= 0.666 or $\frac{2}{3}$

We can confirm this by listing the outcomes that meet the criteria, which are 1, 3, 5 and 6. These four represent $\frac{2}{3}$ of the possible six outcomes, so this agrees with the answer obtained by using the **addition rule**.

While the **addition rule** considers the question of **either** one event occurring **or** another, the **multiplication rule** considers the question of one event occurring **and** another (or others). The rule is used where there is a series of independent events for which each individual probability is known and we want to know the overall probability.

> Crucial concept   According to the **multiplication rule**, if any two events are independent, then the probability of *both* occurring is the product of the separate probabilities:
>
> P(A and B) = P(A) x P(B)

For example, the probability of throwing a die twice and getting a one followed by a four is:

P(1 followed by 4)   = P(1) x P(4)

$$= \frac{1}{6} \times \frac{1}{6} \times \frac{1}{36}$$

> Crucial concept   The **complementary rule**: if there are several different possible outcomes to an event and p_1 = probability of first outcome, ... and p_n = probability of nth outcome, then $p_1 + p_2 + ... + p_n = 1$. In other words, the sum of all the probabilities of all the possible outcomes adds up to 1. The probability of an event **not** occurring is therefore 1 minus the probability of that event.
>
> In general $P(\bar{x}) = 1 − P(X)$, where $\bar{x}$ is 'not X'.

For example, if four dice are thrown, what is the probability of obtaining at least one three? The probability of obtaining at least one three is 1 minus its complement:

P(at least one three) $= 1 - $ P(no threes)

P(no threes)   = P(not three on the first throw and not three on the second ... and not three on the fourth die)

$$= \frac{5}{6} \times \frac{5}{6} \times \frac{5}{6} \times \frac{5}{6} = \frac{625}{1,296} = 0.48$$

P(at least one three) $= 1 - 0.48 = 0.52$

Quick test

1. What are mutually exclusive events?

2. Define the addition and multiplication rules.

Section 3	Combinations and permutations

What are you studying?

In this section we look at the concepts of combinations and permutations which take into account whether the *order* of outcomes is important in determining whether an event has or has not taken place.

How will you be assessed on this?

In any problem involving probability you will be expected to note whether each event you are calculating a probability for requires a specific order or not, and then to use the appropriate approach for that situation.

Suppose that you have three coloured balls in a bag – one red, one blue and one green. If you then take them out of the bag individually without replacing them, the possible results can be shown in a table, as follows:

First ball	Second ball	Third ball
Red	Blue	Green
Red	Green	Blue
Blue	Green	Red
Blue	Red	Green
Green	Blue	Red
Green	Red	Blue

Thus there are three possibilities for the first ball drawn from the bag. Once that ball has been drawn, there are only two possibilities for the second, and then only one for the third. So altogether there are six possibilities, i.e. $3 \times 2 \times 1$.

If there were four balls in the bag, it would become much harder to show this in a table as the number of possibilities would be $4 \times 3 \times 2 \times 1 = 24$, and for five it would be 120. As we are making a distinction based on the order in which the outcomes occur, i.e. (green, blue, red) is different from (green, red, blue) these arrangements are called **permutations**.

> **Crucial concept** The number of **permutations** of n distinct objects is $n!$ (called n factorial), where:
>
> $$n! = n \times (n\text{-}1) \times (n\text{-}2) \times \dots \times 2 \times 1$$

This expression holds true if all objects are selected for each permutation; if there are three balls in the bag we select them individually until there are none left. In some cases we might want to know the number of permutations for selecting a certain number of objects from a larger group of objects, e.g. selecting four letters to form a 'word' from six letters.

> **Crucial tip** You should use a calculator that has the facility to calculate factorials for you. Then you simply press the number followed by the factorial button (usually x!).

> **Crucial concept** The number of different **permutations** of r objects which can be made from n distinct objects (referred to as ^nP_r) is:
>
> $$\frac{n!}{(n-r)!}$$

So, the number of permutations of four letters from a possible six is:

$$\frac{7!}{(7-4)!} = \frac{7!}{3!} = \frac{5{,}040}{6} = 840$$

In some situations, the order in which items are selected may not matter. In this instance, if the result of drawing two balls from a bag is green followed by blue, this is regarded as the same **combination** as blue followed by green.

> **Crucial concept** A **combination** is a selection of items where the order of sequence does not matter. The formula used for calculating the number of combinations is:
>
> $$^nC_r = \frac{n!}{r!(n-r)!}$$
>
> where n is the total number of items and r is the number of items per arrangement.

As an example, if you are attempting an examination paper that consists of eight questions and you are required to attempt five of them, in how many ways can this be done if none of the questions are compulsory? Using the formula:

$$\frac{8!}{5!(8-5)!} = \frac{40{,}320}{720} = 56$$

Quick test

1. Are there more combinations or permutations of the letters 'm, p, a, r, e'?

2. What is 6!?

Section 4   Conditional probability and Bayes' rule

What are you studying?
In this section we look at situations where probability is being calculated on the basis of an extra condition.

How will you be assessed on this?
If a question asks you to calculate the probability of an event, you need to assess whether any conditions are placed on that event, and if so use the appropriate formula

> Crucial concept   **Conditional probability** is the probability associated with combinations of events but given that one of the events has already occurred, and is usually expressed in the form P(A/B), which means the probability of A given that B has already occurred.
>
> $$P(A|B) = \frac{P(A \text{ and } B)}{P(B)}$$

Suppose a toy box contains seven blue dolls and four white dolls. Two dolls are selected without replacement. To find the probability that both dolls are blue we need to find the probability that the first is blue (event B), and the probability that the second is blue **given that the first is blue** (event A).

Our formula can be expressed as P(A and B) = P(A) × P(A|B),

$$= \frac{7}{11} \times \frac{6}{10} = 0.38$$

Bayes' rule (or theorem) is used to work backwards from effect to cause. It can be used where information is given in the form of conditional probabilities and the reverse of these probabilities must be found.

> Crucial concept   The general form of **Bayes' rule** is:
>
> $$P(A|B) = \frac{P(A) \times P(B|A)}{P(B)}$$

Suppose we have a group of students consisting of 40 girls and 60 boys who are given the option of choosing a class in classical or jazz music, and we know that 26 girls and 30 boys have chosen classical. If a student is selected at random and has chosen jazz, what is the probability that the student is a boy? Using Bayes' rule:

$$P(\text{boy}|\text{jazz}) = \frac{P(\text{boy}) \times P(\text{jazz}|\text{boy})}{P(\text{jazz})}$$

$$\frac{0.6 \times 0.5}{(0.4 \times 0.35) + (0.6 \times 0.5)}$$

$$= 0.68$$

Quick test

1. What is conditional probability?

2. Define Bayes' rule.

3. What is the difference between dependent and independent events?

Section 5   Probability distributions

What are you studying?
In this section we will look at how the normal distribution (introduced in Chapter 1) and the binomial distribution can be used to calculate probabilities.

How will you be assessed on this?
You will be expected to be able to use the characteristics of probability distributions to calculate the probability of certain events. This requires an understanding of the characteristics of each distribution – in particular, knowing when to use each distribution – and the ability to use statistical tables to obtain results.

One fundamental distinction is between discrete distributions and continuous distributions. In Chapter 1 we saw that the normal distribution is a continuous distribution. This means it relates to situations such as the length of materials, age of people, etc. In contrast, the binomial distribution (which we will look at in more detail here) deals with situations where there is a number of trials each of which can result in a 'success' or 'failure' – i.e. the results are discrete. The classic example for the binomial distribution is tossing a coin; the only outcomes are 'heads' or 'tails'.

> Crucial concepts **Continuous distributions** apply where data can take on any numerical value. **Discrete distributions** apply where data can only take on specific, fixed values.

In Chapter 1 we looked at the use of charts to represent distributions, and saw that the normal distribution took a symmetrical and bell-shaped curve (see Figure 2.2). We can use the characteristics of this curve to calculate probabilities. As the area under the curve represents the entire population, then the sum of all the probabilities must be 1. By calculating the area under

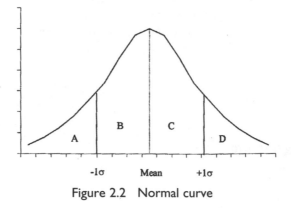

Figure 2.2   Normal curve

different sections of the curve, we can calculate the probability of a randomly chosen item falling within that range. A key relationship here is that between the area under the curve and the standard deviation of the distribution.

Total area = A + B + C + D = 1

Area within 1 standard deviation of the mean = B + C = 68.26% of the area

Area between the mean and plus 1 standard deviation = C = 34.13% of the area

Area greater than mean plus 1 standard deviation = D = 15.87%

Crucial tip	When you are solving problems, it is usually advisable to draw a sketch of the distribution to ensure that you are calculating the correct area.

Statistical tables provide detailed figures for areas under the curve, usually to four decimal places. More information on the use of these tables is provided in Chapters 4 and 5. As an example of the use of such tables, a table showing the area in the tail (area D in Figure 2.2) will have the following entries (note that this is only an extract from the table):

	0	1
0.9	.1841	.1814
1.0	**.1587**	.1562
1.1	.1357	.1335
1.2	.1151	.1131

So if we want to know the probability of a random selection being greater than the mean plus 1 standard deviation, the answer is 15.87% or 0.1587. Similarly, the probability of being greater than the mean plus 1.22 standard deviations is 0.1131. Obviously the full table has a greater range than this, ranging from being greater than the mean (probability 0.5) to the mean plus 2.99 standard deviations. This limit is because in the normal distribution, 99.74% of the area is within 3 standard deviations of the mean, so values beyond that are not usually worth calculating.

Crucial tip	Make sure you know which area of the curve the table you are using refers to. Some show the area in the 'tail' (area D in Figure 2.2) while others show the area between the mean and the tail (area C).

Now let us look briefly at the binomial distribution. As mentioned above, this deals with situations where there are two possible outcomes; a successful outcome 'p', and an unsuccessful outcome 'q'. As there are only two outcomes possible, p + q = 1, or p = 1 − q. As with the normal distribution, there are two main parameters, the mean and the standard deviation:

Mean = np (where n is the number of trials)

Standard deviation $\sqrt{(npq)}$

The simplest way of understanding this distribution is to look at an example. Let's assume that we have a group of eight employees, and we know that on average 75% of employees in the whole company are members of the company pension scheme. What is the expected number of employees that are in the pension scheme from our group of eight, and what is the standard deviation?

Expected number in the scheme = np = 8 x 0.75 = 6 employees

Standard deviation $\sqrt{(npq)} = \sqrt{8 \times 0.75 \times 0.25} = 1.22$ employees

If we wanted to know the probability of selecting exactly four employees who are members of the scheme from a random sample of six employees, we can use the following formula:

> **Crucial tip**
>
> This formula might look a bit daunting, but the good thing is that it can be applied in any situation where you are identifying the probability of a certain number of successes from a specified number of trials, assuming there are only two possible outcomes.

Probability of x successes in n trials = $^nC_x\, p^x q^{n-x}$

$$n = 6$$
$$x = 4$$
$$p = 0.75$$
$$q = 0.7$$

Probability = $^6C_4\, (0.75)^4 \times (0.25)^2$

$$= \frac{6!}{(6-4)! \times 4!} \times 0.316 \times 0.0625$$

$$= 15 \times 0.316 \times 0.0625 = 0.296$$

We have been stressing that the normal distribution is for continuous variables (such as time) and the binomial for discrete variables with two possible outcomes. However, it is generally acceptable to use the normal as an approximation to the binomial, provided that the following circumstances apply:

- n is large and p is close to 0.5;
- both np and nq are greater than 5.

For example, if n = 50 and the probability of failure is 0.38, what is the approximate probability of 39 or more successes? We can use the normal approximation here, so we need to know the mean and the standard deviation:

$$\mu = np = 50 \times (1-0.38) = 31$$

$$\sigma = \sqrt{npq} = \sqrt{50 \times 0.62 \times 0.38} = 3.432$$

What we need to do is compare the desired result of 39 or more successes with the mean of 31 (which is basically the expected result if you perform the trial often enough):

$$\frac{\text{Desired result} - \text{Mean}}{\text{Standard deviation}} = \frac{39-31}{3.432} = 2.33$$

This means that the probability of 39 or more successes lies 2.33 standard deviations above the mean. You may remember that we identified that 99.74% of the area under the curve in the normal distribution lies within 3 standard deviations of the mean. The corresponding percentage for 2 standard deviations is 95.44%, so the probability associated with results **greater than** 2.33 standard deviations above the mean we would expect to be a very small number. By looking up the statistical table we find that the area between the mean and 2.33 standard deviations above it is 0.4901, so 99.01% of the area lies below this. The figure we are after relates to the area in the tail, so we subtract 0.9901 from 1, giving an answer of 0.0099, or approximately one chance in a hundred.

Quick test

1. In what circumstances can the normal distribution be used as an approximation to the binomial?

2. What percentage of the area under the normal curve lies within 2 standard deviations of the mean?

Crucial examples

1. Find the probability of the following (assuming a shuffled pack of 52 cards):

   (a) drawing a jack;

   (b) drawing a jack or king;

   (c) drawing the ace of spades, replacing it and then drawing the same card again.

2. In a class of 30 students there are 18 boys and 12 girls. Ten of the boys own their own car, and four of the girls own a car. If a student is chosen at random, and they do not own a car, what is the probability that the student is a girl?

3. A contestant must choose an item from each of three bags. Each bag contains three balls – red, white and blue. To win, the contestant must select three balls of the same colour. What is the probability of the contestant drawing at least one blue ball?

4. The probability of more than 20 lunch guests at a restaurant on any one day is 0.4. What is the probability of more than 20 lunch guests on more than one day in a five-day week?

5. Explain each of the following terms:

Addition rule	Independent event
Bayes' rule	Multiplication rule
Binomial distribution	Mutually exclusive events
Combinations	Permutations
Complementary probability	Probability
Conditional event	Probability distribution
Conditional rule	Sample space
Continuous distribution	Uncertainty
Dependent event	Venn diagrams
Discrete distribution	

Answers

1. (a) $\dfrac{4}{52}$ or $\dfrac{1}{13}$ or 0.077

   (b) $\dfrac{8}{52}$ or $\dfrac{2}{13}$ or 0.154

   (c) $(\dfrac{1}{52} \times \dfrac{1}{52}) = 0.00037$

2. P(girl and not car owner) $= \dfrac{\text{P(girl and not car owner)}}{\text{P(not car owner)}}$

$$= \dfrac{\dfrac{8}{30}}{\dfrac{16}{30}} = \dfrac{1}{2} \text{ or } 0.5$$

3. P(at least one blue)   = 1 − P(no blues)

   P(no blues)   = P(first not blue and second not blue and third not blue)

$$= \dfrac{2}{3} \times \dfrac{2}{3} \times \dfrac{2}{3} = 0.3$$

   P(at least one blue)   = 1 − 0.3 = 0.7

4. Using the binomial distribution:

   P(0 days) = $^5C_0$ $(0.4)^0 \times (0.6)^5 =$ 0.0778

   P(1 day)   = $^5C_1$ $(0.4)^1 \times (0.6)^4 =$ <u>0.2592</u>

                        <u>0.3370</u>

   P(> 1day) = 1 − 0.337 = 0.663

5. Check your answers against the crucial concepts in the text.

Crucial reading and research

Reading

Curwin, J. and Slater, R. (2002) *Quantitative Methods for Business Decision,* 5th edn. Thomson Learning. See Chapter 8: Probability (pp. 171–84 and 188–90), and Chapter 9: Discrete Probability Distributions (pp. 204–13).

Lucey, T. (1996) *Quantitative Techniques,* 5th edn. Letts Educational. See Chapter 2: Probability and Decision Making (pp. 7–18) and Chapter 4: Statistics – Introduction (pp. 46–64)

Research

You should look out for the use of probability figures in publications such as newspapers and magazines. Note the ways these are used, and try and work out for yourself whether they are being used correctly or not.

There is more detail on the use of probability distributions in Chapters 4 and 5. You may also want to look at other topics that are not covered in this textbook. The Poisson distribution, like the binomial, is a discrete distribution, but it looks at situations where n is large and p is small.

CHAPTER 3

DECISION-MAKING
UNDER UNCERTAINTY

Chapter summary

One of the key roles of managers is making decisions. Usually, when an important decision needs to be made, there is more than one course of action that could be taken, and each course of action can have several different outcomes. Rather than rely on instinct, what was done in the past or some other unreliable approach, it is useful for the manager to have a systematic method for identifying the best available course of action. As well as looking at different decision-making criteria and how to utilise them, we will consider when each approach is most appropriate.

Studying this chapter will help you to:

- calculate and use expected values;
- create decision trees and use them to determine the best course of action;
- use other decision-making rules, i.e. maximin, maximax and minimax regret;
- discuss different attitudes to risk.

Assessment targets

Target 1

The ability to calculate expected values is a necessary skill for both decision trees and other statistical methods. Question 1 at the end of this chapter tests how well you are able to do this.

Target 2

The ability to create and use simple decision trees is fundamental to answering decision tree questions at any level. Question 2 at the end of this chapter tests that you can carry out these basic tasks.

Target 3

Creating and using decision trees involving multiple decisions could form the basis of a full examination question, and takes the topic a stage further than previous assessment targets. At the end of the chapter, Question 3 is demanding, and if you can complete this successfully it indicates that you have grasped the key elements of this topic.

Target 4

Decision trees are the main focus of this chapter, but there are alternative decision rules which are discussed that could appear as supplementary questions in an examination. Question 4 at the end of this chapter contains some brief questions testing your ability to use these decision rules appropriately.

Crucial concepts

These are the key terms and concepts you will meet in this chapter:

Backward pass	Minimax regret
Decision node	Outcome node
Expected values	Risk-averse
Forward pass	Risk-neutral
Maximax criterion	Risk-seeking
Maximin criterion	

Relevant links

As most of the approaches to decision-making in this chapter incorporate probabilities into the information, an understanding of basic probability is assumed, i.e. it is helpful to have covered **Sections 1** and **2** of **Chapter 2** before attempting this chapter. There is also a brief reference to standard deviation, which has been introduced in **Chapter 1**.

Section 1   Expected values

What are you studying?

In this section we will look at how expected values are calculated and how this information should (and, importantly, should not) be used in decision-making.

How will you be assessed on this?

The main importance of expected values in this chapter lies in its application as part of the creation and analysis of decision trees. In order to answer an examination question on decision trees, it is essential that you can calculate expected values accurately and then use this information correctly in determining and explaining a decision.

If a manager is faced with making a decision where there are several different choices and each choice can have more than one outcome, these outcomes can be combined with the associated probabilities (if they are known) to assist the manager in choosing the best option. As an extreme example, let's say you have a friend who bought an old painting for £10 in a car boot sale and sold it an auction a year later for £510. A profit of 5,000% in one year sounds better than the 5% interest offered by the bank. However, the chances of you repeating your friend's amazing success by going to a car boot sale with your £10 are probably very slim. So although the possible return is very high, when combined with its associated probability it might not be a better option than the guaranteed 5% from the bank. This is basically the underlying concept within the expected value approach.

> **Crucial concept**   The **expected value** of a particular action is found by multiplying the value of each of the possible outcomes by their respective probabilities and adding the results together.
>
> $EV = \Sigma px$

> **Crucial tip**   When using expected values, the decision-making criterion is usually to maximise the expected value, i.e. choose the course of action with the highest expected value.

Example

A company is wanting to launch a new product but is unsure which of two possible selling approaches to use, i.e. supermarkets or via their website. Using both outlets is not an option at this stage. With each option, the demand might be low, medium or high, with probabilities of 0.2, 0.5 and 0.3 respectively. If the supermarket approach is used, levels of net income from different levels of demand are estimated as £20,000, £50,000 and £60,000. If the website is used, the estimates are −£10,000 (i.e. a loss), £45,000 and £110,000. We can show the associated expected values in the form of a table:

Demand	Probability	Supermarket		Website	
		Net income	Net income x Probability	Net income	Net income x Probability
Low	0.2	20,000	4,000	−10,000	−2,000
Medium	0.5	50,000	25,000	45,000	22,500
High	0.3	60,000	18,000	110,000	33,000
Total	1.0		£47,000		£53,500

So, as the criterion is the maximisation of expected value, the outlet with the higher expected value will be chosen, which in this case is the use of the website. However, it is important to note the limitations of this approach:

- The expected value is the outcome arising from repeating the action many times. It is an averaging of the possible outcomes after taking probabilities into account.

- The expected value usually does not match any of the possible outcomes. So, for the website, £53,000 is not one of the three possible outcomes.

- The approach is not suitable for one-off decisions because it is based on the law of averages.

- The course of action with the highest expected value (in this case the website outlet) may have potential problems. In this example, if demand turns out to be low, then the website will result in a loss (whereas the supermarket approach would have given a small profit).

- There is an assumption that the probabilities and values can be estimated with some degree of accuracy. In this example, the difference in expected values is £6,500. Minor changes to the probability estimates or the income estimates would significantly affect this difference.

Quick test

1. If a decision has possible outcomes of 100 euros, 150 euros, 250 euros and 300 euros profit, with probabilities of 0.25, 0.2, 0.4, 0.15, what is the expected profit?

(Answer at the end of this chapter.)

Section 2 — Decision trees

What are you studying?
This section looks at more complex decisions than the ones considered in Section 1. Where a number of decisions need to be made in sequence, rather than draw up a simple table, it is usually necessary to create a 'tree' diagram and then identify the expected values that apply.

How will you be assessed on this?
This technique is a suitable focus for a full examination question in which you are presented with a complex set of options, values for outcomes and associated probabilities. The assessment is partly related to your ability to represent the series of options logically (i.e. a test of understanding) and partly to do with the numerical analysis. It is also common to have some testing of your ability to interpret the results and highlight any limitations.

Crucial concept	A **decision tree** is a way of applying the expected value criterion to situations where a number of decisions are made sequentially. The decision alternatives are represented as branches in a 'tree' diagram.

Crucial tip	The first step in analysing any decision-making problem is to identify all the relevant items in the scenario and clarify which are decision points and which are outcomes over which the decision-maker has no control.

Let's consider an example to illustrate how a decision tree is constructed. A computer shop is considering whether to expand its facility to sell additional laptops or PCs. If they sell laptops, they estimate that there is a 60% chance of sales being high, generating profit of £35,000, and 40% of being low with a loss of £5,000. PCs have equivalent estimates of 40% and £20,000 for high sales, and 60% and £1,000 loss for low sales. The first step is to distinguish between decisions and outcomes so that the initial diagram can be drawn accurately.

There is one decision to be taken, i.e. to sell laptops or PCs. If they choose to sell laptops, there are two possible outcomes, i.e. high sales or low sales. And the same two possible outcomes apply to selling PCs. The decision tree can then be drawn from left to right, showing the various decision and outcome points. This stage is referred to as the forward pass (see Figure 3.1).

Crucial concept	The **forward pass** is the process of drawing the logical framework of the decision tree from left to right, showing decisions and possible outcomes.

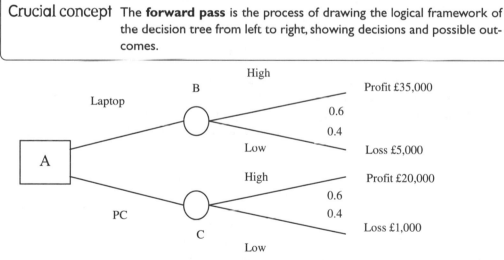

Figure 3.1   Decision tree: forward pass

Crucial tip	Remember that analysing the information in the question and converting that into a logical diagram us usually the difficult part of the decision tree assessment, so it is worth taking time to get this right.

The diagram now shows the single decision, represented by point A in the diagram, and the two outcomes possible for each of the two options, represented by the branches at points B and C. It is important to note the different nature of these points. At point A, the company needs to make a decision as to which branch to follow, laptops or PCs. At points B and C the company cannot influence the outcome, i.e. the next branch is outside their control. The decision tree needs to be drawn in such a way that these points are highlighted as being different, and the use of boxes to represent decision points (or nodes) and circles for outcome points (or nodes) helps to make that distinction.

> **Crucial concepts** A **decision node** is shown in the decision tree as a square and indicates a point where the decision-maker has a choice between different options. An **outcome node** is depicted by a circle and indicates a point where the events depend on probabilities.

We can now use the information to calculate expected values:

Expected value at point B is (0.6 x 35,000) + (0.4 x – 5,000) = 21,000 – 2,000 = £19,000
Expected value at point C is (0.6 x 20,000) + (0.4 x – 1,000) = 12,000 – 400 = £11,600

As there was only one decision point in this problem we could have gone straight to the expected value calculations as we did in Section 1. The example has been used here to illustrate the basics of drawing a decision tree. The true benefits of this technique only become apparent with more complex situations involving more than one decision, so we will look at such an example now.

> **Crucial tip** In decision tree examination questions it is often the case that you are required to work out the profit or loss figures for each possible outcome rather than being given them in the question.

A football club is looking at options for expanding its ground in the context of a ten-year business plan. They are conscious that increasing the capacity does not guarantee additional spectators, but have estimated that there is a 70% chance of a significant increase in attendances if they opt for a new stand. However, if they modify one of the existing stands to accommodate more people, they estimate only a 50% chance of a significant increase. There is the option if they initially modify an existing stand that in two years' time they could add another tier, giving the equivalent of a new stand.

The following estimates have been put together regarding income and costs:

Costs:	Building new stand	£30 m
	Modifying stand	£13 m
	Additional tier	£26 m
Income:	New stand additional annual income	£10 m (high demand)
		£1 m (low demand)
	Modified stand additional annual income	£6 m (high demand)
		£4 m (low demand)
	Combination of modified stand plus additional tier from year 3 would have same income potential as new stand.	

The decision tree is shown in Figure 3.2.

Rather than try and squeeze the net income calculations into the diagram, we will set them out in a table, cross referenced to the outcomes at the right side of the table, i.e. 1 to 6.

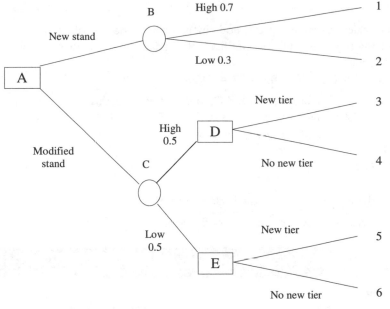

Figure 3.2   Football ground expansion: decision tree

Outcome	1	2	3	4	5	6
Income years 1 and 2	20	2	12	12	8	8
Income years 3 to 10	80	8	80	48	8	32
Initial cost	(30)	(30)	(13)	(13)	(13)	(13)
Additional tier			(26)		(26)	
Net income/(cost)	£70m	£(20)m	£53m	£47m	£23m	£27m

Now that we have worked out the value of each possible outcome, we need to apply this information to the Figure 2.4 along with the probability figures. We do this by working from the right side of the diagram to the left.

> Crucial concept The **backward pass** (or rollback technique) involves working through the decision tree from right to left towards the initial decision node, calculating the EV at each outcome node. At decision points, routes to the outcome nodes with the higher EV are chosen, and other routes from the decision point are blocked off.

Node		£m
B	EV of node B is found by multiplying the probabilities by the net incomes for outcomes 1 and 2 from the table above: 0.7 x £70m x 0.3 x £–20m = £43m	43
D	Decision would be to add the tier as this gives net income of £53m compared with £47m. So 'no new tier' branch can be blocked off.	53
E	Decision would be not to add the tier as this gives net income of £27m compared with a cost of £23m. So 'new tier' branch can be blocked off.	27

Node	£m

C   We can calculate the EV at this node by multiplying the probability by the   40
EV for the branches that have not been blocked off (EV node D is 53, EV node
E is 27), thus:
EV node C = 0.5 x 53 + 0.5 x 27 = £40m

A   We now have EVs for nodes B and C, so the decision at this node is to choose   43
the higher of the two. EV of node B is 43, and EV of node C is 40, so choice is
route to node B, i.e. build the new stand.

Quick test

1. What are the forward pass and the backward pass?
2. How are decision nodes and outcome nodes depicted in a decision tree?

Section 3   Other decision rules

What are you studying?
In this section we will look at a number of different decision-making techniques that employ different criteria, namely minimax, maximax and minimax regret.

How will you be assessed on this?
It is unlikely that a large question in an examination would be devoted solely to any of the techniques discussed in this section. However, they could be combined together, included as an additional task with a decision tree question or used in a multiple choice situation. Also, the issues raised in this section have relevance for interpreting the results of a decision tree, particularly in terms of avoiding risk.

Attitudes to risk

The EV approach uses probabilities and expected outcomes to determine the best course of action, but in some cases might not give an answer that the decision-maker will be happy with. For example, you might use it to compare the cost of an insurance premium with the value of your home and the probability of it burning down. It might appear more cost effective, in terms of EV, not to insure your house, but most people would be unhappy about taking that approach. The decision rules in this section take the attitude to risk into account in the way that the decision criteria are formulated. It is common to look on attitude to risk in three categories:

- **risk-averse** – where the decision-maker looks to keep risk to a minimum;
- **risk-neutral** – where the decision-maker views risk as being neither good nor bad;
- **risk-seeking** – where the decision-maker actively seeks out risky options because there are opportunities for high returns.

Crucial tip	It is usually worth including a reference to risk and different attitudes to risk in any answer to a decision-making question. This includes expected value or decision tree questions that don't include risk as part of the numerical analysis.

Maximin criterion

This is an approach that would be suitable for risk-averse decision-makers. It involves comparing the worst case scenario for each option, looking to avoid options that have the poorest outcomes from this point of view. This approach is sometimes referred to as 'minimax' when looking at costs or loss rather than income or profit, but the essential logic is the same.

> Crucial concept The **maximin criterion** involves selecting the option that will maximise the minimum profits or minimise the maximum losses.

The technique is most easily seen by means of an example.

A small company is looking to acquire a photocopier. The running costs will depend on the volume of use, which cannot be predicted exactly. The manager has identified three possible levels of usage, shown in the table below as low, medium and high. She has also received information from four suppliers allowing her to determine estimated running costs at each level of usage.

Supplier	Low £	Medium £	High £
ABC	1,800	1,800	1,800
XYZ	1,950	1,500	1,600
MNO	2,400	1,350	1,050
RST	500	1,100	2,000

To apply the maximin rule, we need to isolate the worst outcome for each option. These are:

Supplier £	Highest cost £
ABC	1,800
XYZ	1,950
MNO	2,400
RST	2,000

The company would select supplier ABC using this rule, as the worst that could happen is that it costs £1,800. If we selected one of the others, there is a risk that the costs **might** be higher.

Maximax criterion

This also sometimes goes under the name of 'minimin' if considering costs or losses, but essentially the approach is simply to look for the option with the best possible outcome. It is clearly less cautious than the maximin approach, and is therefore more suited to risk-seekers.

> Crucial concept The **maximax criterion** involves selecting the option that will maximise the maximum profits or minimise the minimum losses.

Using the same example, the relevant figures would be:

Supplier	Lowest cost £
ABC	1,800
XYZ	1,500
MNO	1,050
RST	500

Using this rule, the decision would be to ask RST to supply the photocopier. The risk seeker would be happy to take this approach because it gives an opportunity to keep the costs very low.

Minimax regret criterion

This approach considers what might happen if a decision was taken, and then at a later date it was found to be the wrong decision for the circumstances that prevailed. We could work out the level of 'regret' by comparing the cost (or income) resulting from our decision and the cost (or income) that would have been best under the actual circumstances.

> Crucial concept   The **minimax regret criterion** involves selecting the option that will minimise the maximum regret.

In our example, if we selected ABC and the level of usage turned out to be low the costs will be £1,800. We will wish we had chosen RST, at a cost of £500. Our level of regret can be measured as the difference between the two, i.e. £1,300. The minimax regret rule uses this approach to identify maximum regrets for each option, and the decision criterion will be to select the lowest of these. As there are a large number of combinations, the first stage is to compile a regret table, showing the level of regret for each combination. The figures are calculated by identifying the best option under each level of usage and subtracting the cost of this option from each other option in that column. In each case, the best option will have a score of zero, indicating no regret.

Supplier	Low £	Medium £	High £
ABC	**1,300**	700	750
XYZ	**1,450**	400	550
MNO	**1,900**	250	0
RST	0	0	**950**

The maximum regrets therefore are:

Supplier	Maximum regret £
ABC	1,300
XYZ	1,450

MNO	1,900
RST	950

As the company in this case wants to minimise the maximum regrets, the choice would be supplier RST.

Quick test

1. What are the three main categories of attitude to risk?
2. Which would you say was the more pessimistic or cautious approach, maximax or maximin?

Answer to Quick test for Section 1

1. The expected profit is:

Probability	Profit	
0.25	100	25
0.2	150	30
0.4	250	100
0.15	300	45
Expected profit		200

Crucial examples

1. A gambler plays a game in which two cards are drawn from a pack of 52. He is paid £0.20 for each point scored with each card. An ace scores 1 point, cards 2 to 10 score the same number of points as the number on the card, and jack, queen, king each score 11 points. If he pays £15 to enter the game, what is the expected value of playing? (Assume that the first card is replaced in the pack before the second is drawn.)

2. A company is looking to fill a key vacancy for a sales manager and is considering whether to use a specialist recruitment agency or not. The managing director has heard glowing reports from friends who have used a new agency, filling similar positions with high-quality personnel. Enquiries have indicated that using the agency would cost £5,500. In the past, the managing director has used the national press and a specialist magazine to place adverts for this level of staff, spending no more than £3,000 each time. Sometimes, however, the calibre of applicant has been less than he was looking for, and extra costs have been incurred in training the new recruits. This has happened approximately 40% of the time, and training costs have averaged £3,500. What should the managing director decide?

3. SRQ Technology is about spending money on developing an improved version of its best selling items. They estimate that it will cost £1m to carry out the proposed development, and there is a 60% chance that this will lead to a significantly improved product, and a 40% chance of minimal improvement. They will have the option at the end of the development

phase of launching the new product, with marketing casts of £0.5m, or dropping it, with no additional costs. If the product is launched, there is an 80% chance that there will be new competition. Income estimates over the lifetime of the product are as follows:

Improved product, with competition	£10m
Improved product, no competition	£20m
Not improved product, with competition	£4m
Not improved product, no competition	£8m

Draw a decision tree illustrating this problem and use it to determine whether the company should develop the product.

4. An investor is considering three investments, and the following profits and losses have been established:

Market conditions:	Poor	Average	Good
Investment	£	£	£
X	25,000	27,000	30,000
Y	−5,000	5,000	50,000
Z	12,000	28,000	25,000

Which investment should be chosen using the maximin, maximax and minimax regret critiera?

5. Explain each of these terms:

Backward pass	Minimax regret
Decision node	Outcome node
Expected values	Risk-averse
Forward pass	Risk-neutral
Maximin criterion	Risk-seeking
Maximax criterion	

Answers

1. The quickest way to work this one out is to calculate the average score expected from drawing each card. We know for face cards, the score will be 11, and there are 12 of these cards. If we consider the other 40 cards, we know the score can range from 1 to 10, and there is an equal chance for each score because there are four cards for each number. As the distribution is even, we can assume that the average score from these 40 cards is 5.5 points (i.e. the mid point between 1 and 10).

EV for each card drawn = (40/52 x 5.5) + (12/52 x 11) = 4.23 + 2.54 = 6.77 points
EV from playing = (6.77 x 2) − 15 = 13.54 − 15 = − £1.46

2. See the decision tree shown in Figure 3.3

EV at outcome point B = 0.5 x 3,500 + 0.5 x 0 = £1,750

At decision point A, choice between agency costing £5,500 and advert at £3,000 + £1,750, so the managing director should use the advertisement approach.

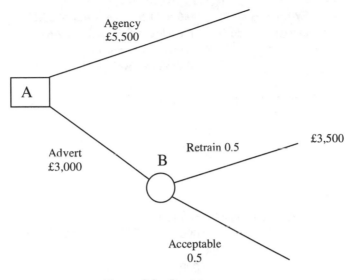

Figure 3.3   Decision tree

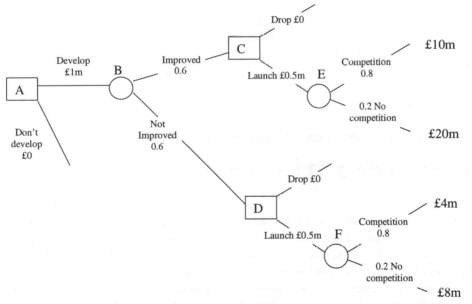

Figure 3.4   Decision tree

3. The decision tree is shown in Figure 3.4.

Backward pass: EV node E $0.8 \times 10 + 0.2 \times 20 = £12m$
                    EV node F $0.8 \times 4 + 0.2 \times 8 = £4.8m$
                    Decision node C   Drop = £0
                                       Launch = $12 - 0.5 = £11.5m$
                                       therefore launch
                    Decision node D   Drop = £0
                                       Launch = $4.8 - 0.5 = £4.3m$
                                       therefore launch

EV node B		$0.6 \times 11.5 + 0.4 \times 4.3 = £8.62m$
Decision node A		Develop = $8.62 - 1 = £7.62m$
		Don't develop = £0
		therefore develop

4. Maximin

Investment	Minimum return
X	25,000
Y	−5000
Z	12,000

Therefore select X.

Maximax

Investment	Maximum return
X	30,000
Y	50,000
Z	25,000

Therefore select Y.

Minimax regret	Poor £	Average £	Good £
X	0	1,000	**20,000**
Y	**30,000**	23,000	0
Z	13,000	0	**25,000**

Therefore select X.

5. Check your answers against the **Crucial concepts** in this chapter.

Crucial reading and research

Reading
Curwin, J. and Slater, R. (2002) *Quantitative Methods for Business Decision,* 5th edn. Thomson Learning. See Chapter 8: Probability, section 8.6 on decision trees (pp. 185–8).

Drury, C. (2000) *Management and Cost Accounting,* 5th edn. Chapman & Hall. See Chapter 12: Decision Making under Conditions of Risk and Uncertainty (pp. 411–29).

Lucey, T. (1996) *Quantitative Techniques,* 5th edn. Letts Educational. See Chapter 2: Probability and Decision Making, (pp. 24–6), and Chapter 3: Decision Trees (pp. 30–8).

Research
There are other related topics that you may wish to look into. The value of perfect information looks at how much it would be worth to acquire perfect information to improve decision-making. Another decision rule not covered in this text is the Hurwicz criterion. This approach takes a weighted average of the best and worst outcomes for each option, with the weights being related to attitude to risk.

CHAPTER 4

STATISTICAL INFERENCE
AND SAMPLING

Chapter summary

Managers and others in organisations use statistical techniques both to **describe** data and to make **inferences** based on it. This chapter deals with the second of these two objectives.

Studying this chapter will help you to:

- describe why it is often necessary to use sample data in preference to data relating to the whole population;
- explain how samples are drawn so that you may rely on their results;
- understand the way in which sample data is related to the corresponding population.

Assessment targets

Target 1

Describe the reasons why organisations take decisions based on samples and the key steps in the process of making statistical inferences. This is tested in Questions 1 and 2 at the end of this chapter.

Target 2

Describe the main forms of sampling. See Questions 3 and 4 at the end of this chapter.

Target 3

Estimate population parameters given knowledge of the sample statistics. Question 5 at the end of this chapter covers this point.

Crucial concepts

These are the key terms and concepts you will meet in this chapter:

Best estimate	Parameter
Cluster sample	Point estimate
Confidence	Sampling distribution
Confidence interval	Simple random sample
Controlled sample	Standard normal distribution
Hypothesis	Statistic
Inference	Stratified random sample
Normal distribution	Tail of distribution

Relevant links

The material in this chapter forms the basis for much of the work on hypothesis testing in **Chapter 5**. You will also find that it draws on the ideas of probability contained in **Chapter 2** where you learned about the binomial distribution.

Section 1	Objectives, process and role of statistical inference

What are you studying?

This section describes why we would wish to use statistical inference and how it can help with estimating and making decisions. It also sets out a model of the process of making inferences that will act as a basis for chapters later in this book on estimation and hypothesis testing.

How will you be assessed on this?

You may be asked to describe the purpose and process of statistical inference and to describe the main forms of sampling that may be undertaken.

Managers in business generally use statistics for two purposes: to describe data and to make **inferences** about the data. You can think of inferences like predictions that we use to help in making decisions. Because so much of the data that managers use is **sampled** from a (usually very large) population a key problem is deciding what can be said about the population on the basis of what we know from the sample. Making these statements, and assessing how reliable they are, is at the heart of statistical inference.

> Crucial concept **Statistical inference** is the process of making statements about a population based on knowledge of the data contained in a sample drawn from that population.

You might ask why we need to take samples – after all isn't it better to deal with the data in the whole population? The short answer is that it is often either impossible or impractical in a business setting to analyse the data in a population. Even where it might be possible to obtain whole population data it will almost always be less expensive to collect data from a sample. If you can make reliable inferences from a relatively small sample then why go to all of the expense of surveying the whole population and probably coming to the same conclusions?

Sometimes it is simply not possible to conduct a survey of the whole population. A manufacturer of light bulbs would probably be interested to know the mean time to failure of his product. Determining this by testing each one to destruction would be highly accurate but he wouldn't stay in business for long!

Sampling can often produce an instantaneous result that would not be possible by any other means. A steel-maker is concerned to know about the purity of the steel that he is making. Drawing samples from the production line can give this information many times a day even though it might take some hours or days to complete the finished product.

There are therefore lots of good reasons why you might want to take samples from a population. But how do we actually go about the process of making inferences?

1. We define the question that we are trying to answer or the problem that we are trying to solve.

2. We determine the data that we will need to collect to form our sample in order to answer our question or solve our problem.

3. We collect our data and analyse it.

4. We make our inferences.

5. We assess how **reliable** our inference is.

Every problem in inferential statistics follows that same five-step process. It's set out in the diagram in Figure 4.1.

It's important to point out that while statistical inference can help the decision-maker at all five stages in the process, the final stage, actually making the decision, will almost always involve the exercise of judgement. That may be for a variety of reasons: the statistical data may only be part of the story, there may be other data that needs to be taken into account, or the decision-maker may use experience and intuition to help make the decision. Good decisions in business are almost always based on good data, but are not an automatic by-product of the analysis of that data.

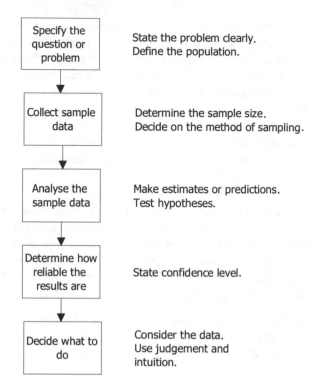

Specify the question or problem	State the problem clearly. Define the population.
Collect sample data	Determine the sample size. Decide on the method of sampling.
Analyse the sample data	Make estimates or predictions. Test hypotheses.
Determine how reliable the results are	State confidence level.
Decide what to do	Consider the data. Use judgement and intuition.

Figure 4.1   Making inferences

When we want to make a statistical inference we do so because there are 'things' that we want to know about our population. We might want to know the average weekly spending on leisure pursuits, for example, or the average value of an invoice outstanding. The 'things' in the population that we want to know about are called **parameters** of the population. When we take a sample and measure the 'thing' in the sample we call the 'thing' that we measure a **statistic**.

> Crucial concept   The characteristics of the populations that are of interest to us are
> called the **parameters** of the population. When we talk about those
> same things in a sample we use the term **statistic**.

So the mean of a population is a parameter and the mean of a sample is a statistic.

When we use a statistic to make inferences about the corresponding parameter the first thing we need to ask ourselves is whether we can use the statistic immediately to estimate the parameter or whether we need to make some adjustment to it before doing so. The answer to this question will depend on how good an estimator of the parameter the statistic is. In this context 'good' is quite closely defined – we need only have a broad understanding of what is meant. A statistic is a 'good' estimator of the corresponding parameter if:

- when we use it many times, on average it will equate to the parameter; and
- if we take larger samples, the variance of the sample gets smaller.

In addition we say that a statistic is the **best estimate** of the parameter if estimates made using this statistic are better, on average, than those made using any other.

> **Crucial concept** A statistic is a **best estimate** of a population parameter if it meets the criteria for being a good estimator and if estimates made using this statistic are on average better than those made using any other possible estimator.

In very many business situations we are interested in estimating the population mean from knowledge of the sample mean. It can be shown that the sample mean provides a 'best estimate' of the population mean.

> **Crucial tip** The sample mean is a best estimate of the population mean.

Another aspect of populations that is often of interest to the decision-maker is the variance (or its close cousin, the standard deviation). You might think that the sample standard deviation might be a best estimate of the population standard deviation. Sadly, not! The sample standard deviation usually underestimates the population standard deviation, and therefore we usually need to make an adjustment, based on the size of the sample. For small samples our best estimate of the population standard deviation is $s \times \sqrt{n/(n-1)}$. Making this adjustment will always make the sample standard deviation bigger. However the amount by which it makes it bigger gets smaller as the sample size increases, and after a time it becomes really too small to worry about. For all practical purposes most statisticians would accept that forgetting about the adjustment for samples larger than 30 is perfectly acceptable, and even the most niggardly will concede that no adjustment is needed for samples larger than 50!

> **Crucial tip** If you are free to choose the size of the sample that you plan to take then choose one larger than 30. This will avoid the need to adjust the sample standard deviation and simplify the arithmetic.

When we use a sample statistic to estimate the value of the population parameter we are making what is known as a **point estimate**. Now unless we are very lucky our point estimate is unlikely to be spot on the parameter. You will see later therefore that one of the important aspects of using statistics to make inferences revolves around the idea of **confidence** and **confidence intervals**. We will be more precise in what we mean by that later, but for the moment you can think of it in two ways:

- how **certain** you can be that the estimate is correct, expressed in terms of the probability that the estimate is right; and

- as a **range** of values within which you are confident that the true value of the parameter lies.

> **Crucial concept** A single estimate of a population parameter is called a **point** estimate. When we make a point estimate we will often want to provide a measure of the **confidence** that we have in the accuracy of that estimate.

A second use of statistical inference that we will develop in the next chapter has to do with testing **hypotheses** about the population. A hypothesis is a belief about the population that we wish to test. For example, we might hypothesise that adult males spend more on certain items than adult females and wish to test whether that is true or not. One way of doing this is to take two samples, one of adult males and the other of adult females and measure how much each group spends on the items in question. We could easily calculate the average spending by each group, and would almost certainly discover that the amounts were different. The question we then need to ask ourselves is whether the difference is in some sense 'big enough' to support our hypothesis that the two groups have different spending habits. You will discover in the next chapter that statistical inference can help here, by providing you with a technique that will allow you to answer that question whilst at the same time knowing how likely you are to be wrong.

> **Crucial concept** When we put forward a theory or belief about some population of interest then we are effectively stating a **hypothesis** about that population. Statistical inference can be used to test that hypothesis with the aim of helping us to decide whether or not it is likely to be true.

One key aspect of making inferences based on samples is the process that we use to form the sample. How can we ensure that we take a 'proper' sample that will form a sound basis for our subsequent analysis? The answer to that question depends on a number of factors. One is the size of the population. Perhaps surprisingly the size of the population doesn't usually matter provided that it is much larger than the size of the sample. A properly constructed sample of 1,000 from a population of 50,000,000 is just as reliable as a similarly sized sample taken from a population of 1,000,000. However, a characteristic of the population that does matter is its **variance**. If the population variance is very large then this may compromise the reliability of data taken from samples. A large variance implies that the data are spread out and this will increase the chance of us taking a sample that is very unrepresentative. There is almost always nothing we can do about the population variance and we often have no information about it. In such circumstances we can do nothing other than use what we know about the sample variance (or more commonly the sample standard deviation) to make statements about the population.

> **Crucial tip** Take a factor of 20 as being the threshold for determining whether the population is sufficiently bigger than the sample size, i.e. as long as the population is at least 20 times bigger than the sample, population size doesn't matter. If this is not the case then there is a technique (discussed in the next chapter) to deal with this.

Another factor that affects the reliability of our inferences is the kind of sample that we take. Our aim is to generate a sample that is representative of the population that we are interested in. There are a number of ways of doing that, although they can generally be grouped into **random** and **controlled** sampling methods. When a statistician talks about taking a random sample they will usually be referring to following a carefully defined process designed to ensure that every item chosen has the same chance of being chosen as any other, and that choosing any one item does not in any way affect the chance that you will choose another. A random sample drawn in this way is known as a **simple random sample**.

> **Crucial concept** A **simple random sample** is one drawn so that each element has an equal probability of being selected.

When drawing a simple random sample it is theoretically necessary to draw from an infinitely large population. However, these are rare in the business world and in practice it is usually good enough that the population be very large compared with the size of the sample (20 times bigger or more). Where this is not so then it is usually sufficient to sample **with replacement**, i.e. each time a member of the population is withdrawn it is (either literally or figuratively) 'thrown back' so that its withdrawal does not affect subsequent probabilities. If sampling with replacement is not appropriate then it is possible to make an adjustment to the sample results to reflect this.

Where it is not possible or desirable to take a simple random sample then a **controlled sample** may provide more representative results. With a controlled sample the population is organised in some way before the random sample is taken. There are a number of forms of controlled sampling methods: they are all designed to produce samples that are representative of the underlying population, sometimes at less cost then using simple random sampling.

> Crucial concept A **controlled** sample is one where the population is structured in some way before the sample is taken. In well designed samples the data is finally drawn randomly, however the initial structuring may have been done.

Stratified random sampling is a form of controlled sampling that is often used to obtain sample data, sometimes at much less cost than using simple random sampling.

> Crucial concept **Stratified random sampling** separates the population into non-overlapping segments or strata that reflect important characteristics of the population. Once the strata have been identified samples are drawn at random from each stratum.

Stratified random sampling is often used where the population consists of a number of groups that are different but where there is a high degree of similarity within groups. Such a sampling method can produce more reliable estimates than simple random sampling although it requires special techniques to form the strata and analyse the results.

Cluster sampling is another method used to help keep down the cost of sampling. In some circumstances it may be very expensive to undertake a simple random sample.

> Crucial concept A **cluster sample** is obtained by randomly selecting from the population a set of sample elements called clusters and then conducting a complete census within each selected cluster.

Quota sampling is another form of sampling that you may have come across. This is where the interviewer is told how many people with the necessary characteristics must be interviewed but beyond that they may at least attempt some element of randomness in their selection. Quota sampling and other forms based on non-random designs should only be used where the aim is to make descriptive statements about the sample without drawing inferences about it. If the aim is to make inferences then some form of random sampling should be used.

Quick test

1. What is the purpose of statistical inference?
2. Why is it necessary to sample data from a population?
3. What are the five steps involved in solving a statistical problem?

4. I want to sample from my local population and therefore choose a simple random sample from the local telephone directory. Is this likely to produce a sample that is free from bias?

5. You intend to use sample data to make inferences about some population. Name three factors that will influence the reliability of the sample data.

6. Describe three forms of sampling and how they may be used.

7. The sample mean is a good estimator of the population mean. True or false?

8. The sample standard deviation is the best estimate of the population standard deviation. True or false?

Section 2 — The normal distribution

What are you studying?

This section describes the **normal** distribution – this is very important one in statistical inference.

How will you be assessed on this?

This material is required to enable your understanding of what follows. It is unlikely that you will be assessed on the concepts relating to probability distributions. However, you will be tested on your ability to apply this knowledge to the more practical situations that you will encounter later in this chapter and in the chapter on hypothesis testing.

Imagine that you obtained data on the height of all females in the country. If you plotted a frequency distribution for this data the resulting chart would look very similar to Figure 4.2.

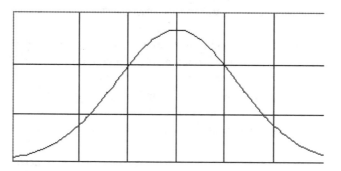

Figure 4.2   Frequency distribution

The heights have been plotted on the x-axis and the frequencies on the y-axis. The chart shows that most people cluster around the middle of the distribution but there are a relatively small number who are either much shorter than average or much taller than average. The distribution shown in the chart occurs so frequently that it has a name: the **normal** distribution. It has a characteristic mound shape and is centred on its mean. In addition, if we calculated the standard deviation of the distribution we would find that nearly all of the values (more than 99% of them in fact) would lie within 3 standard deviations either side of the mean.

> Crucial concept The **normal distribution** is theoretically perfectly bell- or mound-shaped. Many real life variables are distributed normally or approximately normally.

Now in real life there are an infinite number of normal distributions, each corresponding to a variable of interest. Mathematicians have recognised this and therefore have offered us a 'typical' normal distribution called the **standard** normal distribution. It has a mean of 0 and a standard deviation of 1 and the area under the curve, which sums to 1, has been extensively tabulated. Its value lies in the fact that we can transform any real-life normal distribution into the standard normal distribution with a relatively simple formula that we will learn about shortly. For the moment, however, we need to explore further what we know about this standard normal distribution before we see how we can use it to make estimates of population parameters.

> Crucial concept The **standard normal distribution** is a theoretical normal distribution with mean of 0 and standard deviation of 1.

Each point on the x-axis may be expressed in terms of the number of standard deviations away from the mean. For example, Figure 4.3 shows the points that are 1, 2 and 3 standard deviations away from the mean on both sides.

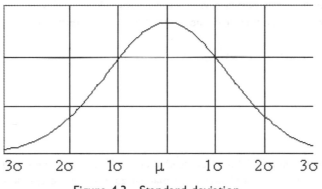

Figure 4.3   Standard deviation

Mathematicians have tabulated these and other values so that you can look up a table and tell how much of the total area will be contained by any multiple or fraction of standard deviations. Because the curve is symmetrical about its mean it is usually enough to tabulate the values in one half. Most books on statistics will contain a version of this table: if you were to consult such a table you would find that:

- 0.3413 of the total area lies between the mean and +1 standard deviation;
- 0.4772 of the total area lies between the mean and +2 standard deviations;
- 0.4987 of the total area lies between the mean and +3 standard deviations.

Given the symmetry of the curve we can develop this to say that:

- 0.6826 (0.3413 x 2) of the total area will lie between the mean and ± 1 standard deviations;
- 0.9544 (0.4772 x 2) of the total area lies between the mean and ± 2 standard deviations;
- 0.9974 (0.4987 x 2) of the total area lies between the mean and ± 3 standard deviations.

These statements can also be made in terms of percentages of course: the second statement just made tells us that over 95% (95.44%) of the total area is contained within 2 standard deviations either side of the mean, for example.

In real life we need to convert any normally distributed variable to the standard one, so that we can use the tabulated values to get areas under the curve of our real life variable. We do it by transforming our variable into the standard normal variable, using the following formula:

$$z = \frac{x - \mu}{\sigma}$$

Crucial tip   A real life variable x may be transformed into the standard normal variable z using the formula: $z = \dfrac{x - \mu}{\sigma}$

Here z is the standard normally distributed variable, x is our variable, μ is our population mean and σ is our population standard deviation. Why this works isn't important for you to understand: how to use it is, and that's what we are now going to learn.

Imagine we have our table of heights from the start of this section. We have calculated the mean and the standard deviation: let's say the mean is 1.55 m and the standard deviation is 12 cm. How can we work out the area under the curve for values of our variable, height? For example, what is the area under the curve between our mean height 1.55 m and, say, 1.80 m? To answer this question we need to transform our variable into the standard normal variable using the formula. So:

$$z = \frac{x - \mu}{\sigma}$$
$$= \frac{1.80 - 1.55}{0.12}$$
$$= 2.08$$

This tells us that a height of 1.80 m expressed in terms of our variable is the same as a value of 2.08 expressed in terms of the standard normal variable. What we are doing here is a bit like converting currencies into some 'standard' currency. For example, if our standard currency were the • then:

- $2 might be worth • 1.70
- £4.50 might be worth • 2.69

and other currencies could be similarly converted into the •.

If we know that a height of 1.8 m is the same as 2.08 in 'standard normal speak' then if we want to know the area contained between the mean and 1.8 m then that's the same as knowing the area contained between the mean and a z-value of 2.08, which we can tell from tables. Using tables we can see that the area between the mean and 2.08 is 0.4812 so we immediately know that the area between our mean, 1.55, and 1.8 is also 0.4812.

At this stage you might still be wondering about the value of knowing areas under curves, whether they are our curves or the standard normal curve. Think about what we have just learned: in our (hypothetical) example of heights we know that just over 48% of the area under our curve lies between the mean and a height of 1.8 m. We can therefore say that the **probability** of occurrence of a height in the range 1.55–1.8 m is just over 0.48. Using the symmetry of the curve we can also say that the probability of someone being 1.8 m **or less** is 0.98. We get this from the fact that the area to the left of the mean is 0.5 and we have just calculated the area from the mean up to 1.8. Adding these two together gives us 0.98 therefore. This is the same as saying that the chance of a member of our population being no taller than 1.8 m is 0.98. We can also say something else using this knowledge and what we know about probability. If the chance of someone being as tall as 1.8 m is 0.98 then the chance that a member of our population is taller than 1.8 m is 1 − 0.98 = 0.02 or 2%. Knowing about areas under the standard normal distribution therefore lets us make statements about probabilities in any real-life normal distribution.

The tables that give areas under the standard normal distribution come in two basic 'flavours':

- some show the area under the curve between the mean and the z-value;
- some show the area under the curve to the right of the z-value.

This is illustrated in diagrammatic form in Figure 4.4.

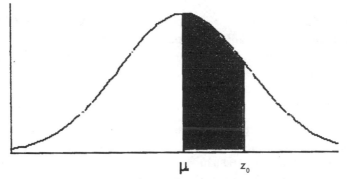

Figure 4.4   Area between mean and z-value

This is an example of the first 'flavour' of table. It shows the area under the normal curve between the mean and the required z-value. An extract from such a table might look like this:

z_0	.00	.01	.02	.03	.04	.05	.06	.07	.08	.09
1.1	.3643	.3665	.3686	.3708	.3729	.3749	.3770	.3790	.3810	.3830
1.2	.3849	.3869	.3888	.3907	.3925	.3944	.3962	.3962	.3997	.4015
1.3	.4032	.4049	.4066	.4082	.4099	.4115	.4131	.4131	.4162	.4177
1.4	.4192	.4207	.4222	.4236	.4251	.4265	.4279	.4279	.4306	.4319
1.5	.4332	.4345	.4357	.4370	.4382	.4394	.4406	.4406	.4429	.4441

The second form of presentation of the table might look like Figure 4.5 and the tabulated data would show the area under the curve to the right of the stated point.

These tables can be used in a number of ways:

- To determine the area under the curve between the mean and any given z-value. For example, if we want to know the area between the mean and z = 1.46 then we read down the z_0 column until we come to 1.4 and then across the first row to .06 and read off the value at the intersection. In this case this is 0.4279.

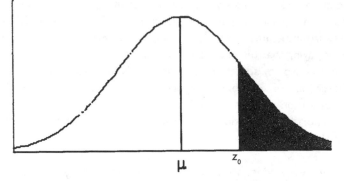

Figure 4.5   Area to the right of the z-value

- To find the z-value that corresponds to a given area between the mean and that value. For example, what is the z-value that contains an area of 0.3907 between itself and the mean? Scan through the cells of the table to find 0.3907. We can see that it lies in the third row and fifth column and that the corresponding z-value is 1.23.

- To find the area under the curve beyond a given z-value. For example, what is the area under the curve corresponding to $z > 1.28$? We can see that the area between the mean and $z = 1.28$ is 0.3997. The area to the right of the mean contains half of the total area under the curve and so the area beyond $z = 1.28$ must be $0.5 - 0.3997$, i.e. 0.1003.

Using the symmetry of the normal curve we can answer some other questions.

- What z-value results in an area of 0.8030 **around** the mean? An area of 0.8030 around the mean will have half of that value on each side of the mean. We therefore need to find the z-value that corresponds to half of 0.8030, i.e. 0.4015. Scanning the table again tells us that the z-value is 1.29 and therefore the range in question is $-1.29 \leq \mu \leq 1.29$, i.e. $\mu \pm 1.29$.

- What area is contained in the range $\mu \pm 1.41z$? Reading the z column to 1.4 and across to the column containing .01 gives the intersection 0.4207. Since this represents the area to the right of the mean up to $z = 1.41$ it must also represent the area to the left of the mean as far as $z = -1.41$. Therefore the answer to the question is 0.4207×2, i.e. 0.8414 or 84.14%.

Familiarity with these tables is important and you should ensure that you can use them quickly and confidently.

> Crucial tip   Practise using both forms of the standard normal table and make sure that you can answer questions about the areas under the curve using both forms.

The areas under the standard normal distribution beyond a stated z-value are often referred to as the **tails** of the distribution.

> Crucial concept   The areas beyond a stated z-value are referred to as the **tails of** the distribution.

Let's look at an example.

The market for executive cars is highly competitive, and consumers are becoming much more conscious of 'green' factors such as recyclability and fuel consumption. Competition is particularly keen in the 'mid-range' sector, where published manufacturers' figures show average fuel consumption of 25.5 mpg and a standard deviation of 4.5 mpg. Fuel consumption is known to be a normally distributed variable. The chief executive officer (CEO) of Luxury Limos plc intends that the company's new model should offer better fuel consumption than 95% of the competition. What target should they set for the engineers to achieve?

To answer this question it helps to see that what our CEO is saying is that they want the fuel consumption of the company's new model to lie in the upper tail of the distribution that marks the 5% point (100% - 95%). Often a diagram helps, and Figure 4.6 illustrates the area we are interested in.

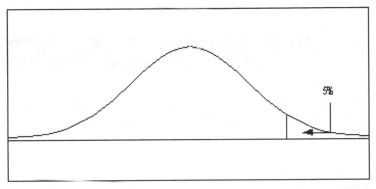

5%

Figure 4.6 Area of interest

As Figure 4.6 shows we want to find the z-value that will mark off areas of 95% and 5%: our CEO wants the fuel consumption for the new model to lie in this upper tail of the distribution. The form of the table that shows the areas in the tail of the distribution seems the most appropriate here. When we scan through the body of the table we see that the area that we are looking for, 0.005, doesn't appear in the table. We can find an area a bit bigger than this, 0.0505, and one a bit smaller, 0.0495, with z-values of 1.64 and 1.65. But what about the area in between? We need to estimate the z-value for the area in question that lies between 0.0505 and 0.0495. The simplest way to do this is to assume that the relevant area lies exactly in the middle and that therefore the corresponding z-value is 1.645.

Having worked out the value of the standard normal variable that leaves an area of 5% in the right tail of the distribution we need to translate that back into our real-life variable. We can use the formula used to translate real-life into normal speak to go in the opposite direction, as follows:

$$z = \frac{x - \mu}{\sigma}$$

$$1.645 = \frac{x - 25.5}{4.5}$$

$$1.645 \times 4.5 = x - 25.5$$

$$x = (1.645 \times 4.5) + 25.5 = 32.9$$

So, if our CEO wants to be confident that the new model will have better fuel consumption than 95% of the competitors they should ask the engineers to design a vehicle with a fuel consumption of 32.9 mpg or better.

Quick test

1. What proportion of the area under the standard normal distribution lies within ±2 standard deviations of the mean?

2. What is the mean of the standard normal distribution?

3. How do you convert a 'regular' variable into a standard normal one?

4. What do you call the areas in the extreme parts of the standard normal distribution?

Section 3   Sampling and sampling distributions

What are you studying?
In the previous chapter we learned that it is often necessary to make inferences about some aspect of a population based on data gathered from a sample. So how do we extend what we know about the sample to the whole population? This section answers that question.

How will you be assessed on this?
This material is required to enable your understanding of what follows. It is unlikely that you will be assessed on the concepts relating to probability distributions. However, you will be tested on your ability to apply this knowledge to the more practical situations that you will encounter later in this chapter and in the chapter on hypothesis testing.

Imagine that we are given some data taken from a sample of 100 25-year-olds, drawn at random from our population, which is all 25-year-olds in the country that we live in. When we calculate the average or **mean** amount spent on social and leisure activities each week by that group of 100 it comes to £53. Is it reasonable to assume that the average amount spent each week by the whole population is also £53?

Imagine that we take a sample of some given size from our population and calculate the mean of the characteristic in question. We note down our result and then throw our sample data back into the population. We then draw a second sample of the same size and again note down the mean. And again we throw the data back. And we keep on doing that *ad infinitum*. We end up with a very large number of measurements. Many would differ from each other although there would also be some similarities. If we then calculated the probability distribution of our sample mean (called the **sampling distribution of sample means**) we would see that it was normal.

Our distribution of sample means has a mean that is equal to the population mean. Our distribution also has a standard deviation. This standard deviation is usually known as the **standard error** of the mean rather than the standard deviation but it amounts to the same thing. The standard error of the mean is equal to the population standard deviation divided by the square root of the sample size.

> **Crucial concept** If we take a random sample of n measurements from a population with mean μ and standard deviation σ the **sampling distribution of the sample mean** $\bar{x}$ will have a mean and standard deviation:
>
> $$\mu_{\bar{x}} = \mu \text{ and } \sigma_{\bar{x}} = \frac{\sigma}{\sqrt{n}}$$

In most practical business situations the sampling distribution of sample means will be normally distributed **even if the population data is not**.

These results can also be shown to apply to other statistics. In particular we are often interested in saying something about the proportion of our population possessing some characteristic. Where we are interested in proportions (and therefore the population follows a **binomial distribution**) then we can express the equivalent result as follows:

> **Crucial concept** If a random sample of n observations is taken from a binomial population with proportion p the **sampling distribution of the sample proportion**:
>
> $$\hat{p} = \frac{x}{n}$$
>
> will have a mean and standard deviation:
>
> $$\mu_{\hat{p}} = p \text{ and } \sigma_{\hat{p}} = \sqrt{\frac{pq}{n}}$$

This allows us to say that our best estimate of the population proportion p is our sample proportion $\frac{x}{n}$. It also tells us that the standard deviation of the sampling distribution of the sample proportion $\sigma_{\hat{p}}$ is calculated by taking the square root of the product of p and q (where $q = 1 - p$) divided by the sample size. In practice we do not usually know the population proportion p and so estimate it using the sample proportion $\hat{p}$.

Quick test

1. What do we call the standard deviation of a sampling distribution?
2. Under what conditions is the sampling distribution of sample means normally distributed?
3. What is the best estimate of the population proportion, expressed in terms of the sample proportion?

Section 4 | **Estimating means and proportions from large samples**

What are you studying?
This section describes how to make estimates of the population mean and the population proportion based on knowledge of the sample statistics and the standard normal distribution. Throughout this chapter we assume that we are working with large samples, where this is

defined as being of size greater than 30. There are special techniques for making estimates based on small samples which we will cover in a later chapter. Also, unless stated otherwise, it is assumed that the samples are drawn from a population that is many times larger than the sample, or that sampling is with replacement. 'Many times larger' is taken to mean that the population is at least 20 times the size of the sample.

How will you be assessed on this?
You may be asked to estimate the value of a population parameter such as the mean or a proportion, and/or to provide a confidence interval within which this estimate is likely to lie.

What we have learned so far helps us to make estimates provided that we are working with normally distributed variables. If we sample repeatedly from a normally distributed population then the sampling distribution of sample means will be normally distributed (this is true even if the sample is small). If the population is not normal then the sampling distribution of sample means will be approximately normally distributed, and the approximation will improve as the sample size increases. This means that, provided the population is 'large' we can use the results of our large random sample to make statements about the population **whatever its distribution**.

We know that the sample mean is a reliable estimator of the population mean. When we use the sample mean to make a single estimate of the population mean we are using it as a point estimator.

A point estimate may well be what our decision-maker wants. However, often he or she will also want to know something about the range within which the true value of the population mean might lie. What we really want to do is give an estimate of the **confidence interval** in which the population mean is likely to lie. Such a statement might be of the form 'the best estimate of the population mean is 103.9 kg. The 95% confidence interval for this estimate is 98.4 kg to 109.4 kg'. In round terms we are saying that we are 95% certain that the mean lies between 98.4 and 109.4.

> Crucial concept   The **confidence interval** is a range within which the population parameter is estimated to lie. It is usually expressed with a stated degree of confidence, often 95% or 99%.

How do we calculate the confidence interval? We use what we have learned about the standard normal distribution and what we already know about the reliability of the sample standard deviation as an estimator of the population standard deviation. What do we know?

- We know that the sample mean is a reliable estimator of the population mean. Our best point estimate of the population mean is therefore the sample mean.

- We know that the sample standard deviation is not a reliable estimator of the population. However, we also know that if we multiply it by $\sqrt{n/n-1}$ then the result will be a reliable estimator.

Now follow this line of argument carefully:

- From what we have learned about the standard normal distribution we know that 95% of the distribution lies within ±1.96 standard deviations of the mean.

- Our sample mean is one value from the whole range of values that make up the sampling distribution of the sample mean. That sampling distribution is normally distributed. Its mean is μ, the population mean. Its standard deviation (called the standard error) is $\sigma/\sqrt{n}$ where n is the sample size.

- The first statement tells us that our sample mean lies within ±1.96 standard errors of the population mean. But if this is so then the population mean must also lie within ±1.96 standard errors of the sample mean.

If our best estimate of the population mean is the sample mean $\bar{x}$ then all of this means that our best estimate of the interval within which the population mean lies, with 95% confidence, is $\bar{x}\pm1.96\,\sigma/\sqrt{n}$ i.e. we can be 95% confident that our population mean lies within that range.

We (probably) do not know σ, the population standard deviation. No matter – we can use the sample standard deviation as our best estimate provided that we adjust it as described earlier. So, restating our confidence interval in a way that involves things that we can calculate gives $\mu=\bar{x}\pm1.96s/\sqrt{n}\times\sqrt{n/(n-1)}$. We can simplify this a little by noticing that $\sqrt{n}$ occurs in both the numerator and the denominator of the expression and so we can eliminate it to give $\mu=\bar{x}\pm1.96s/\sqrt{n-1}$.

This expression is known as the **95% confidence interval** for the estimate of the population mean, μ. The limits at each end of the interval are known as the **95% confidence limits**. It is quite common to use 95% in business applications although we are free to choose whatever confidence level is appropriate in the circumstances. Another common level is 99%: using tables to obtain the appropriate z-value gives us $\mu=\bar{x}\pm2.58s/\sqrt{n-1}$. This is the **99% confidence interval** for our estimate of the mean.

> Crucial tip
>
> The 95% and 99% confidence intervals are used so frequently in making estimates that it's worth memorising them. The z-value for the 95% interval is ±1.96 and the z-value for the 99% interval is ±2.58.

The confidence interval for the estimate of the population mean that we have derived in this way is known as a **two-tailed** confidence interval. The interval is taken to lie around the mean and therefore the area under the curve that we are not interested in is divided equally between both tails of the distribution.

> Crucial concept
>
> A **two-tailed** confidence interval places the estimate of the population mean in the centre of the interval and divides the area that remains equally between the two tails of the distribution.

We've done enough theorising for the moment: let's see how the formula works in practice.

A local authority Direct Service Organisation operates an asphalt production plant which has an average daily yield as measured over a 50-day period of 871 tonnes with a standard deviation of 21 tonnes. What is the interval estimate of the true average daily yield?

The parameter of interest in this case is the population mean: we want to say something with confidence about the mean of the total output from the plant, based on what we have measured over the sample period. We can reasonably assume that the population will be normally distributed, and even if it isn't then statistical theory tells us that the sampling distribution will be approximately normal.

We have been given the mean of the sample data, which is 871 tonnes. From what we have already learned we know that the sample mean is the best point estimate of the population mean: now we need to calculate a confidence interval within which that best estimate is likely to lie. Before we can do that we need to decide how confident we want to be: let's choose 95%. We use our formula $\mu = \bar{x} \pm 1.96s / \sqrt{n-1}$ and substitute the known value of the sample mean $\bar{x}$, which is 871, the sample standard deviation s, which is 21, and the sample size, n, which is 50. Doing this gives:

$$\mu = \bar{x} \pm 1.96s / \sqrt{n-1}$$
$$= 871 \pm 1.96 \times 21 / \sqrt{50-1}$$
$$= 871 \pm 5.88$$
$$= (865.12, 876.88)$$

This tells us that the 95% confidence interval for the mean amount of asphalt produced by the plant in a day is the range 865.12 – 876.88. If we want to talk in everyday terms then we can tell the plant manager that he can be 95% confident that the plant is producing between 865 and 877 tonnes a day.

In most real-life situations you will be estimating the population parameter, e.g. the mean, because you do not know what it is. You will probably not know the population standard deviation either, and will therefore be using the techniques described in this section. However, on those probably quite rare occasions when you do know the population mean or standard deviation then you should use it in preference to the sample statistic.

> **Crucial tip** If you know one or both of the population parameters then you should use them.

So far we have considered the sampling distribution of sample means. Often, however, we will be interested in characteristics of our populations which may more naturally be expressed as proportions. The proportion of employees earning more than £15,000 p.a., the proportion of invoices sampled which is in error; and the proportion of stock items with no recent movement are all examples from business life where the statistic of interest is the proportion rather than the mean. In such circumstances we can use a technique that is very similar to what we have just developed for means.

Again assuming we take random samples, if the sample proportion is p then the best estimator of the population proportion is also p. The 95% confidence interval for the population proportion is given by:

$$p \pm 1.96 \sqrt{\frac{pq}{n}}$$

where p is the (measured) proportion of the sample having the characteristic that we are interested in, q is $1 - p$ and n is the sample size. Now when working with proportions we are using a **binomial** variable. The binomial distribution can be difficult to work with because of the burden of working out the binomial coefficients in anything other than the most trivial of cases. You learned in the chapter on probability that we can use the normal distribution to approximate the binomial provided that certain conditions are met. We therefore need to ensure that those conditions are met if we want to estimate the value of a population proportion based on sample data. Since we want to use a particular normal distribution, the standard normal distribution, to approximate the binomial distribution then we require that

$p \pm 2\sqrt{\dfrac{pq}{n}}$ lies in the interval (0, 1).

Crucial tip	When estimating the value of a population proportion based on knowledge of a sample, check first of all that the sample proportion plus or minus twice the standard error lies in the interval (0, 1).

Let's look at an example.

A candidate in a local election wants to estimate the share of the vote that he is likely to get. He samples 100 voters and learns that 62 are likely to vote for him. What is the 95% confidence interval for the estimate of the proportion of the whole electorate that is likely to favour him with their vote?

We first of all check that we may use the normal distribution and calculate:

$p \pm 2\sqrt{\dfrac{pq}{n}}$ where $p = 0.62$, $q = 1 - 0.62 = 0.38$ and $n = 100$

This comes to (0.52, 0.72) and is therefore comfortably within our required range of (0, 1). Applying the formula for the 95% confidence interval gives us:

$p \pm 1.96\sqrt{\dfrac{pq}{n}} = 0.62 \pm 0.095 = (0.525, 0.715)$

Our candidate may therefore reasonably assume that he will get between 52% and 71% of the vote.

Quick test

1. What do we call the interval formed to contain our best estimate of a population parameter?
2. What is a point estimator?
3. Define 'confidence interval'.
4. What is the 95% confidence interval for the estimate of the population mean?
5. What is the z-value that corresponds to the 95% confidence interval? The 99%?

Crucial examples

1. Why do organisations use sampling to take decisions?
2. What are the main steps in the process of statistical inference?
3. List the main forms of sampling.
4. What is the difference between random sampling methods and controlled sampling methods?
5. A random sample of annual earnings of 100 staff working in a college of further education

showed an average of £17,750 with a sample standard deviation of £900. What is the 99% confidence interval estimate of the true average annual salary?

Answers

1. Organisations use sampling because:

   • it may be impossible or impractical to use whole population data;

   • they wish to reduce the cost of making decisions;

   • sampling provides an instantaneous measure.

2. See Figure 4.1.

3. The main forms of sampling are:

   • simple random sampling;

   • quota sampling;

   • cluster sampling;

   • stratified random sampling.

4. With random sampling methods each sample element has the same chance of being selected. With controlled methods the population is organised or grouped in some way before the sample is drawn, at which point a random sample may then be taken from each group. The theory on which statistical inference is based depends on the samples being drawn at random.

5. We want to form a 99% confidence interval within which the mean salary lies: from tables we know that the z-value corresponding to this is 2.58 and so we can use our formula as follows:

$$\mu = \bar{x} \pm 2.58 s / \sqrt{n-1}$$
$$= 17750 \pm 2.58 \times 900 / \sqrt{100-1}$$
$$= 17750 \pm 233.36$$
$$= (17,516, 17,984)$$

if we talk in round £. We could tell the college management that they can be 99% certain that the average member of staff is earning between £17,516 and £17,984 per annum.

Crucial reading and research

Reading

Curwin, J. and Slater, R. (2002) *Quantitative Methods for Business Decision*, 5th edn. Thomson Learning. See Part 4: Statistical Inference, Introduction (pp 239–425) and Chapter 11: Confidence Intervals (pp. 245–70).

Lewis, J.P. and Trail, A. (1999) *Statistics Explained*, Addison-Wesley. See Chapters 16, 21 and 22.

Lucey, T. (1996) *Quantitative Techniques*, 5th edn. Letts Educational. See Chapter 5: Statistics – Statistical Inference (pp. 72–82).

Mendenhall, W., Reinmuth, J.E. and Beaver, R.J. (1993) *Statistics for Management and Economics*, 7th edn. Duxbury Press. See Chapters 6–8 and 17.

Research

In this chapter we have touched only briefly on the subject of sampling methods and you may wish to follow up the reading references to develop your understanding of this aspect.

CHAPTER 5

HYPOTHESIS TESTS

Chapter summary

In the previous chapter you learned how to make estimates of the values of population parameters based on knowledge gained from samples. Often a decision-maker is not concerned to know the value of a parameter but rather whether or not it is what he or she expected. For example, a sawmill may make boards to be used in flooring. The specification for the boards might require that they be at least 2.5 metres long. The manufacturer would wish to test samples of boards from time to time to determine the extent to which they met this criterion, i.e. they were at least 2.5 m long. The actual length may not matter so long as each board met the minimum standard. Decisions of this kind are generally referred to as **hypothesis tests** and in this chapter you will learn how to conduct them. While the procedure for carrying out these tests will be quite general you will find that there is an important difference if we are undertaking tests based on large samples than if the sample is small.

Studying this chapter will help you to:

- explain the role of hypothesis tests in making inferences;
- conduct a hypothesis test;
- understand the kind of errors that may arise when carrying out a hypothesis test.

Assessment targets

Target 1

Perform a hypothesis test based on large or small samples and describe the kind of errors that may arise when conducting a hypothesis test. Questions 1 and 2 at the end of this chapter test this.

....

Crucial concepts

These are the key terms and concepts you will meet in this chapter:

Acceptance region   Student's distribution
Alternative hypothesis   Test statistic
Hypothesis test   Type I error
Null hypothesis   Type II error
Rejection region

....

Relevant links

This material is a development of what has been learned about estimating and therefore the chapters on that topic should be regarded as a prerequisite to studying this one.

....

Section 1	The nature of hypothesis tests

What are you studying?

This section describes the purpose of a hypothesis test and the general structure of such a test. It also explains the kinds of error that may arise in conducting a hypothesis test and the effect they have on the way in which the test is carried out.

How will you be assessed on this?

You may be asked to explain the process of carrying out a hypothesis test and to describe what can be done to manage the errors that might arise.

> Crucial concept   A **hypothesis test** is a test of an assumption (the hypothesis) designed in such a way that you may either reject or not the hypothesis in favour of some alternative hypothesis. The hypothesis to be tested is referred to as the null hypothesis and the other hypothesis is the alternative hypothesis.

In the sawmill example given at the start of this chapter, the null hypothesis would be that the boards were at least 2.5 m long and the alternative hypothesis would be that they were less than 2.5 m. We would conduct the test by drawing a (random) sample of boards and calculating the average length. We would then work out the probability of getting an average of this size, based on the fact that the averages would be normally distributed. If we find that this probability is in some sense very low then that will lead us to believe that our boards were not in fact at least 2.5 m long. That is the essence of our hypothesis test.

A hypothesis test is a test of the value of some statistic. In the sawmill case this was the mean length of a board, although you will also learn how to test proportions, differences between means and differences between proportions. Sample data is used to calculate a single value, the test statistic, that will be used as a basis for making the decision to reject or not.

> Crucial concept Sample values are used to calculate a single number that acts as a decision-maker. This single value is called the **test statistic**.

Our test statistic (for large sample tests) will be the by now familiar z-value, and using our knowledge of the normal distribution we will divide the values that our test statistic may take into a **rejection region** and an **acceptance region**. If the calculated value of the test statistic is 'big enough' it will lie in the rejection region and this will give us enough confidence to reject the null hypothesis in favour of the alternative hypothesis. If the value of the test statistic is not 'big enough' then it will fall into the acceptance region, which will give us no reason to reject the null hypothesis.

> Crucial concept The **rejection region** represents the values of the test statistic that support rejection of the null hypothesis. The **acceptance region** corresponds to values that support acceptance of the null hypothesis. If the calculated value of the test statistic lies in the rejection region we will reject the null hypothesis.

The procedure that you will learn to apply will be as follows:

1. State the null hypothesis (referred to as H_0).
2. State the alternative hypothesis (H_a).
3. Calculate the test statistic.
4. Determine the rejection region.
5. Reject or do not reject the null hypothesis, according to the value of the test statistic and the rejection region.

We have said that we will reject the null hypothesis if the calculated value of the test statistic is in some sense 'big enough'. What do we mean by that? Well, 'big enough' will be defined in terms of how many standard errors away from the mean the test statistic lies. From our knowledge of the normal distribution we know that about 95% of it lies within 2 standard deviations of the mean, and almost all of it lies within 3 standard deviations. We will define a critical value of our test statistic in terms of how far it lies from the mean, and use this to define the rejection and acceptance regions. If the calculated value of the test statistic lies in the rejection region this will give us the confidence to say that it is unlikely that the null hypothesis is true and so we will reject it.

Hypothesis tests allow us to make statements about probabilities rather than certainties. If we reject the null hypothesis we have to accept the fact that we might do so when we ought not to. Alternatively we might fail to reject the null hypothesis when we ought to have done. In both of these cases we commit an error, as we can see from the following table:

| Our decision may be to | In reality the null hypothesis may be | |
	True	False
Reject the null hyupothesis	Type I error Probability α	Correct decision Probability $1-\beta$
Not reject the null hypothesis	Correct decision Probability $1-\alpha$	Type II error Probability β

> **Crucial concept** If we reject the null hypothesis when we really ought not to have done then we commit a **Type I error**. The probability of making such an error is denoted by α.
>
> If we do not reject the null hypothesis when we ought to have done we make a **Type II error**. The probability of doing that is denoted by β.

When we carry out hypothesis tests you will see that we can always specify α in advance. We will therefore always know the probability of making a Type I error. However, in general terms, the probability β, that of failing to reject the null hypothesis when it is false, is much more difficult to calculate than α. It depends among other things on how close to the hypothesised value of the parameter the true value lies. If we cannot quantify β then we do not know the probability of making a Type II error. Since this error arises when we accept the null hypothesis when we ought not to have done so then we get round the difficulty by never doing that. Therefore a hypothesis test can have only one of two possible outcomes:

- we may reject the null hypothesis in favour of the alternative, with probability of error α; or
- we do not reject the null hypothesis.

Quick test

1. What are the steps involved in conducting a hypothesis test?
2. What kinds of error might we make in carrying out a hypothesis test?
3. What are the possible outcomes of a hypothesis test?
4. How do we decide where to locate the rejection region?

Section 2 — A large sample hypothesis test of a population mean

What are you studying?
This section describes how to carry out a hypothesis test of a population mean, based on the results obtained from a large (>30) sample.

How will you be assessed on this?
You may be asked to state the elements of a hypothesis test and to determine whether or not you may reject the null hypothesis based on information contained in a large sample.

Consider again the local authority Direct Service Organisation producing asphalt for use in road-making from Chapter 4. Samples of output from the plant over a period of 50 days showed a mean output of 871 tonnes with a sample standard deviation of 21 tonnes. Test the hypothesis that the average daily yield is actually 880 tonnes on the basis of this sample.

We set out the steps in our hypothesis test in the following way.

State the null hypothesis $H_0 : \mu = 880$

State the alternative hypothesis $H_a : \mu \neq 880$

Calculate the value of the test statistic

We want to calculate the z-value corresponding to our sample output of 871 tonnes and our sample standard deviation of 21 tonnes. This will then allow us to determine the probability of getting a value different from that. We'll play safe and use the theoretically correct estimate of the population standard deviation in calculating the standard error:

$$z = \frac{\bar{x} - \mu}{s/\sqrt{n-1}}$$

$$= \frac{871 - 880}{21/\sqrt{49}}$$

$$= \frac{-9}{3}$$

$$= -3$$

Determine the rejection region

We will set α equal to 0.05 so that we may be 95% confident in our decision. From tables we know that this corresponds to a z-value of ± 1.96. We will therefore reject the null hypothesis if the calculated value of our test statistic is less than −1.96 or more than +1.96 (we want to detect differences that are significantly less than or significantly greater than the hypothesised value here).

Decide

Our calculated value of the test statistic, −3 is much smaller than −1.96. We may therefore reject the null hypothesis in favour of the alternative.

> **Crucial tip** Practise using a structured and standard approach to the steps in an hypothesis test. This will help to avoid errors and ensure that you set out all of the steps clearly.

Quick test

1. What is the formula for the test statistic when carrying out a hypothesis test of a mean?
2. Under what circumstances may we reject the null hypothesis?

| Section 3 | A large sample hypothesis test of a population proportion |

What are you studying?

This section describes how to carry out a hypothesis test of a population proportion, based on the results obtained from a large (>30) sample. It will follow broadly that procedure described for carrying out the equivalent test for population means.

How will you be assessed on this?

You may be asked to state the elements of a hypothesis test and to determine whether or not you may reject the null hypothesis based on information contained in a large sample.

A manufacturer of baby food intends to launch a new product. He knows from previous market research that 1 in 10 consumers favour his existing product and wishes to conduct some market research to find out whether consumers are likely to prefer the new one. From taste tests he establishes that, from a sample of 300 prospective purchasers, 36 (12%) say they prefer his new product. Do the results from this sample provide convincing evidence that consumers are likely to favour the new product over the old one?

We follow the same pattern as we did for the hypothesis test involving the mean. However, we need to use a different test statistic:

$$z = \frac{p_s - p_0}{\sqrt{\dfrac{p_0 q_0}{n}}}$$

where p_s is our sample proportion, p_0 is our hypothesised proportion, (what we think the population proportion is) and the remaining variables have the usual meanings. Our null hypothesis is that there is no difference between the proportion of consumers who favour the new product and those who favour the existing one, i.e. $H_0 : p = 0.1$, and the null hypothesis that we want to test is that the proportion of consumers who prefer the new product is greater than 0.1, i.e. $H_a : p > 0.1$. In this case we will assume that we are only concerned with detecting a value of p greater than 0.1 and so we will conduct a one-tailed test. So, follow the drill:

State the null hypothesis	$H_0 : p = 0.1$
State the alternative hypothesis	$H_a : p > 0.1$
Calculate the value of the test	$z = \dfrac{p_s - p_0}{\sqrt{\dfrac{p_0 q_0}{n}}}$ $= \dfrac{0.12 - 0.10}{\sqrt{\dfrac{0.1 \times 0.9}{300}}}$ $= 1.15$
Determine the rejection region	We will use the 'usual' 95% confidence level. Since we are conducting a one-tailed test we will place all of the rejection region in the upper tail of 5%. From tables we can see that the critical value of z for which 5% of the distribution lies in the upper tail is 1.645. (We should be becoming quite familiar with these values by now.)
Decide	The calculated value of our test statistic at 1.15 is less than the critical value of 1.645 and so we have no basis for rejecting the null hypothesis.

So, do we accept the null hypothesis, that there is no difference in consumer preference for the two products? No, for the reasons that we described earlier. It is possible that, in rejecting the null hypothesis, we have made a mistake. We can only make statements of this kind with a stated degree of probability. We set up this test to give us only a 5% chance that we would reject the null hypothesis if it was true (commit a Type I error) , and were unable to do so. However, we do not know the probability of making the 'other' kind of error – accepting the null hypothesis when it is false. Most rational decision-makers would wish to know the likelihood of being wrong when they make a decision, and since we cannot tell them that in this case then we act conservatively. Rather than positively accepting the null hypothesis we say that we have no reason to reject it.

In the example just quoted we used the normal approximation to the binomial distribution. We know that to be able to do this we require that $p \pm 2\sqrt{pq/n}$ lies in the interval (0, 1). We ought to calculate that for our example, to be sure that we may use the approximation. Doing the calculation we find that the relevant interval is (0.06, 0.14) which is comfortably within the interval (0, 1).

There is a second complication that can arise when we use the normal distribution to approximate the binomial. Doing this tends to underestimate the actual values and so we ought to make the correction for continuity.

In our example we might well have used a value of 0.115 (11.5%) and so we ought to consider values in the range 11.5% to 12.5%, i.e. 0.5% either side of the measured value. Now taking 12.5% would move our sample mean further away from the hypothesised one, which would be pushing it in the direction that would favour rejecting the null hypothesis. That would distort our calculation, and so we take the lower value, conservatively placing the sample mean closer to the hypothesised one. In the calculation that we did we would therefore use $0.115 - 0.1$ on the numerator. However, you ought to be able to see that if we did this there would be even less evidence to reject the null hypothesis than was the case when we used our 'rounded' method.

In practice when doing calculations of this kind you are usually safe in using the actual sample value. However, if it looks like a close decision as to whether you should reject the null hypothesis or not then you may wish to recalculate the test statistic using the 'precise' value for the sample proportion before deciding.

> ### Crucial tips
>
> When performing a hypothesis test of a sample proportion use the measured sample value to calculate the test statistic. If it appears that the calculated value is very close to the critical value then recalculate the test statistic before deciding whether or not to reject the null hypothesis. In recalculating, adjust the sample proportion by 0.5 so as to bring it closer to the hypothesised value, to be conservative in your judgement.
>
> It is always correct to make the correction for continuity. If you are comfortable in using it then you should do so in all cases. However, if you do not make it, and the value of the test statistic is significantly different from the critical value, you will almost always make the correct decision.

Quick test

1. What is the formula for the test statistic for a hypothesis test of a population proportion?

2. Under what circumstances may we accept the null hypothesis?

3. What conditions do we require to use the normal approximation to the binomial distribution?

4. What correction might we have to make when using the normal approximation to the binomial distribution? Do we always have to make it?

Section 4 — A large sample hypothesis test of the difference between two means

What are you studying?
This section describes how to carry out a hypothesis test of the difference between two means.

How will you be assessed on this?
You may be asked to state the elements of a hypothesis test and to determine whether or not you may reject the null hypothesis based on information contained in a large sample.

We quite commonly wish to make statements about the difference between two means. The procedure for making hypothesis tests of this kind is very similar to what you have seen previously in this chapter and so we will go straight to an example.

The National Logistics Company wants to decide whether to adapt its current fleet of vehicles to run on liquefied petroleum gas (LPG), to reduce running costs. It chooses a random sample of 100 vehicles from its fleet and converts them, and, over a period of time, compares their running costs to those of a similarly sized randomly selected sample of conventionally fuelled vehicles. It found that the LPG fleet had running costs of 11.9p per mile with a standard deviation of 1.8p, and that the conventionally fuelled vehicles had a running cost of 12.4p per mile with a standard deviation of 1.9p. Does this present enough evidence to suggest that LPG is a more economical fuel?

If we designate the mean running cost of LPG powered vehicles as μ_1 and those of conventional vehicles as μ_2 then we can state the null hypothesis as follows:

$$H_0 : \mu_1 - \mu_2 = 0$$

and test it against the alternative hypothesis, that LPG is cheaper.

$$H_a : \mu_1 - \mu_2 < 0$$

Note that this is a one-tailed test since we really wish to detect situations where LPG is less costly than conventional fuels. We will test at the 95% significance level, which gives a critical value for the test statistic of 1.645. (We are placing all of the rejection region in the left-hand tail.) The formula for the test statistic is a little more complicated than we have seen so far because of the presence of terms representing two samples, but the principle of the test and the basic procedure is the same as we have used up to now. The test statistic is given by:

$$z = \frac{(\bar{x}_1 - \bar{x}_2) - (\mu_1 - \mu_2)}{\sqrt{\frac{s_1^2}{(n_1 - 1)} + \frac{s_2^2}{(n_2 - 1)}}}$$

Let's calculate the value of the test statistic:

$$= \frac{(11.9 - 12.4) - 0}{\sqrt{\frac{1.8^2}{99} + \frac{1.9^2}{99}}}$$

$$= \frac{-0.5}{0.263}$$

$$= -1.90$$

We can see from this that the calculated value of the test statistic −1.90 is less than the critical value of −1.645 and therefore we may reject the null hypothesis with confidence. The chance of us being wrong in saying that LPG fuelled vehicles are more economical to run than conventional ones is less than 5%.

Quick test

What is the formula for the test statistic when making a hypothesis test of the difference between two means?

Section 5 — A large sample hypothesis test of the difference between two proportions

What are you studying?
This section describes how to carry out a hypothesis test of the difference between two population proportions, based on the results obtained from a large (>30) sample.

How will you be assessed on this?
You may be asked to state the elements of a hypothesis test and to determine whether or not you may reject the null hypothesis based on information contained in a large sample.

We have so far considered the situation where we want to carry out a hypothesis test of a mean, a proportion and the difference between two means. We can use a similar approach to test a hypothesis about the difference between two sample proportions: we can test whether some observed difference between two sample proportions give us enough evidence to support the view that there is really a significant difference in the population as a whole. In most practical situations we are concerned to determine whether the two samples really belong to the populations that have the same proportion of the characteristic in question, and so we'll concentrate on that situation here.

The Statistical Survey Society carries out a survey of the customers of two bars in a local town. The aim of the survey is to decide whether or not there is any evidence to support the view that one or the other attracts a predominantly female clientele. The well conducted survey shows that of the 76 customers using Bar A 19 are female, while 26 of the 89 customers of Bar B are female. Is there any evidence to suggest that one or other of the bars seems to attract a greater proportion of female customers?

First of all let's note that we are being asked to test whether one proportion is greater than another. That means we need to conduct a one-tailed test and that therefore we will locate all of our rejection region in the upper tail of the distribution. We will test at the 5% level, which means a z-value of 1.645.

From what we have seen so far it ought to be clear that our calculation of z involves a formula that expresses the difference between what we know and the null hypothesis as a proportion of the standard error of the appropriate sampling distribution. We therefore need to know how to calculate the standard error of the difference between two proportions. We have already seen that for a single proportion this is given by $\sqrt{\dfrac{pq}{n}}$ where p represents the population proportion or our best estimate of it. When we have two proportions the standard error is given by:

$$\sqrt{\frac{\hat{p}_1\hat{q}_1}{n_1} + \frac{\hat{p}_2\hat{q}_2}{n_2}}$$

The 'hat' symbols (carets) are used to remind us that we are referring to sample data.

Now we pointed out at the start of this section that it is quite common for us to be testing a hypothesis that the two population proportions are equal. If that is the case then $p_1 = p_2 = p$ and our best estimate of p is obtained by pooling the data from each sample. However, rather than taking a simple average of the two proportions we allow for the fact that the two sample sizes might be different, and use the sample size to 'weight' the calculation of the pooled proportion. Our pooled estimate of the population proportion is given by:

$$\hat{p} = \frac{\hat{p}_1 n_1 + \hat{p}_2 n_2}{n_1 + n_2}$$

In many practical situations we can simplify this formula. Observe that:

$$\hat{p}_1 = \frac{x_1}{n_1}$$

where x_1 is the number of items in the sample whose size is n_1 and $\hat{p}_2 = \frac{x_2}{n_2}$. If we substitute for $\hat{p}_1$ and $\hat{p}_2$ in our 'hatted' equation for the standard error using this then we get:

$$\hat{p} = \frac{\frac{x_1}{n_1} \times n_1 + \frac{x_2}{n_2} \times n_2}{n_1 + n_2} = \frac{x_1 + x_2}{n_1 + n_2}$$

This is rather simpler to calculate, although the first version makes it plainer that the pooled estimate is based on a weighted average of the two sample proportions. We'll use the simple version for calculations.

Having simplified the formula for estimating the population proportion we can restate the standard error as:

$$\sqrt{\frac{\hat{p}\hat{q}}{n_1} + \frac{\hat{p}\hat{q}}{n_2}} = \sqrt{\hat{p}\hat{q}\left(\frac{1}{n_1} + \frac{1}{n_2}\right)}$$

Putting all of this together gives us the formula for calculating the value of the test statistic, z:

$$z = \frac{\hat{p}_1 - \hat{p}_2}{\sqrt{\hat{p}\hat{q}\left(\frac{1}{n_1} + \frac{1}{n_2}\right)}}$$

Now back to our example. We have our sample evidence that shows that 25% ($\frac{19}{76}$) of the customers of Bar A and just over 29% ($\frac{26}{89}$) of those of Bar B are female. We want to test the hypothesis that Bar B attracts a greater proportion of female customers than Bar A. We will therefore test the null hypothesis:

$$H_0 : p_1 - p_2 = 0$$

against the alternative:

$$H_a : p_1 > p_2$$

where we have chosen to represent the proportion of customers using Bar B as p_1. Note that this is a one-tailed test. We will set the probability that we make a Type I error (α) at 5% and determine from tables that the z-value corresponding to this is 1.645. We will therefore reject the null hypothesis if the calculated value of the test statistic is greater than this critical value.

The difference between the two sample proportions is $(0.2921 - 0.25) = 0.0421$ which gives us the numerator in our expression for the test statistic. The denominator is the standard error which is given by:

$$\sqrt{\hat{p}\hat{q}\left(\frac{1}{n_1} + \frac{1}{n_2}\right)}$$

We need to calculate $\hat{p}$ using our formula:

$$\hat{p} = \frac{x_1 + x_2}{n_1 + n_2}$$

which gives 0.2727 and so $\hat{q}$ is 0.7273. Plugging these values into our equation for the standard error gives 0.0696 and so dividing the top half by the bottom half gives 0.6049. This is clearly less than the critical value of 1.645 and so we have no reason to reject the null hypothesis. Keep in mind that this does not prove that there is no difference: it simply does not gives us enough evidence to suggest that there is.

Quick test

1. What is the formula for the test statistic when making a hypothesis test of the difference between two means?

Section 6 — Student's t-distribution and small samples

What are you studying?
In what has gone before we have assumed that the samples on which we wanted to base our estimates, or test our hypotheses, were large in statistical terms. We'll remind ourselves here that large means greater than 30 and that some statisticians would put that at greater than 50. There are some real-life situations where we have to work with small samples. The work we have done so far has been on the basis that we have large samples and so we need an alternative technique, based on the t-distribution.

In this section we will concentrate solely on means and differences between means. It is really only when working with these two parameters that the issue of small samples arises.

How will you be assessed on this?
You may be asked to make an estimate, or conduct a hypothesis test, based on a small sample using the t-distribution. You may also be asked to comment on your results and to explain them.

When we discussed estimating and hypothesis testing based on large samples we were able to make progress because the test statistic z was normally distributed under repeated sampling. When the sample is small we cannot use z, however, because under these circumstances z is not normally distributed. We therefore need to use a different test statistic. When our sample is small we use the test statistic:

$$t = \frac{\bar{x} - \mu}{s/\sqrt{n-1}}$$

This test statistic has what is known as **Student's t-distribution**.

Crucial concept The test statistic $t = \dfrac{\bar{x} - \mu}{s/\sqrt{n-1}}$ is known as Student's t. Under repeated sampling it has a distribution that is mound-shaped, symmetrical about a zero mean, and that depends on the value of n.

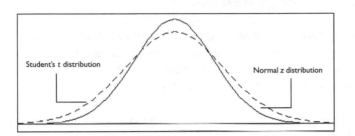

Figure 5.1   Comparison of Student's t-distribution and the normal distribution

Student's t distribution looks a bit like the normal distribution, although it is much more variable. A comparison of the two might look as in Figure 5.1: the t-distribution is the one with the dotted line.

As with the standard normal distribution z, tables of critical values of t have been drawn up. There is one important difference between the t-tables and the z-tables however. Tables of points under the t-distribution require you to know how many **degrees of freedom** apply. The concept of degrees of freedom is a rather difficult one to explain in non-mathematical terms and therefore we will simply explain how to calculate it. For making estimates or testing hypotheses relating to means, the number of degrees of freedom is simply the size of the sample less one, i.e. degree of freedom = $n - 1$

So, in a sample of size 23 there would be 22 degrees of freedom; in a sample of 11, 10 – and so on.

An extract from a table of percentage points of the t-distribution might look like this:

$\alpha =$	0.10	0.05	0.025	0.01	0.005	0.001	0.0005
$\nu = 26$	1.315	1.706	2.056	2.479	2.779	3.435	3.707
27	1.314	1.703	2.052	2.473	2.771	3.421	3.690
28	1.313	1.701	2.048	2.467	2.763	3.408	3.674
29	1.311	1.699	2.045	2.462	2.756	3.396	3.659
30	1.310	1.697	2.042	2.457	2.750	3.385	3.646

Like the table of z-values this shows the proportion of the area under the standard t-curve that lies above the stated value. The top row ($\alpha =$) shows percentage points, in this case from 0.10 (10%) through to 0.0005 (0.05%). The leftmost column shows the degrees of freedom. In this excerpt these start at 26 (the symbol ν is the Greek letter pronounced 'new' that is commonly used to represent the degrees of freedom). If you compare the t-value for $\alpha = 0.05$ with 30 d.f. (degrees of freedom) found at the intersection of the third column and the last row you will see that it is 1.697. If you compare this with the corresponding z-value of 1.645 you will perhaps see why many statisticians choose 30 as the boundary between large and small samples. The two values are very close to each other, within 3% or so, and get progressively closer as n gets larger.

Using the t-distribution to make estimates and test hypotheses is very similar procedurally to using the z-distribution. We must, however, ensure that we take into account the degrees of freedom involved. Let's look at an example.

The proofreader checking this manuscript decides to take a random sample of seven pages from each chapter of the first draft and counts the number of errors found. If she finds an average of 11 errors per chapter, with a sample standard deviation of 3, what is the 95% confidence interval for the number of errors in the whole first draft of the book?

We first of all note that we are working with a small sample (7) and that we are being asked to calculate a 95% confidence interval for the mean number of errors in each chapter. In our work on large samples we saw that the 95% confidence limits for the mean were given by $\mu = \bar{x} \pm 1.96 s/\sqrt{n-1}$. The '1.96' here came from the table of z-values for $\alpha = 0.025$ (2.5% of the total error of 5% in each tail) and so we need to find the corresponding t-value. We have a sample size of 7 and so we know that there are 6 (7 − 1) degrees of freedom. Looking up $\alpha = 0.025$ for $v = 6$ d.f. gives us 2.447. We may therefore say, with 95% confidence, that the mean number of errors per chapter lies in the interval $\left(\bar{x} - 2.447\, s/\sqrt{n-1}, \bar{x} + 2.447\, s/\sqrt{n-1}\right)$, which is the interval (8.00, 17.00) rounding to 3 decimal places. Doing the same calculation using the z-distribution would have given an interval of (8.60, 13.40), which is rather narrower than the correct answer. This illustrates the greater variability of the t-distribution.

Let's look at an example of testing a hypothesis about a mean based on small sample data.

The mean length of iron bars produced in a steelworks should be 1.5 metres. A random sample of 11 bars is taken and the mean length found to be 1.44 metres with a sample standard deviation of 0.04. Test the hypothesis that the manufacturing process is in control.

As with hypothesis tests involving large samples we need first of all to be clear on what we are testing. We would (presumably) be as concerned to find that the bars being produced were over length as under length, which suggests that we want to carry out a two-tailed test. We therefore define our null hypothesis as follows

$H_0 : \mu = 1.5$

and the alternative hypothesis:

$H_a : \mu \neq 1.5$

We have a sample size of 11, which means 10 d.f. We are interested in the 5% significance level which, for a two-tailed test with 10 d.f., gives a t-value of 2.228. We therefore calculate the test statistic:

$$t = \frac{\bar{x} - \mu}{s/\sqrt{n-1}}$$

which gives −4.74 to 2 decimal places. This is clearly much greater in absolute terms than the critical value of 2.228 and so we reject the null hypothesis.

When carrying out a small sample hypothesis test of the difference between two means we require that the two population variances be equal (or nearly so) for the test to be appropriate. This may sound restrictive although in practice this is not unusual. In any event, we may rely on work that has been done that suggests that if the larger sample variance is not more than about 3 times the smaller one, we may use this method.

In testing an hypothesis about the difference between two means we use the test statistic:

$$t = \frac{(\bar{x}_1 - \bar{x}_2) - D_0}{s\sqrt{\dfrac{1}{n_1} + \dfrac{1}{n_2}}}$$

The form of the test statistic presents us with something of a dilemma. It involves s, which is our best estimate of the population standard error, and we have two candidates in the sample standard deviations s_1 and s_2 from our two samples. Which of these should we use for s? Well the answer is that we use both of them! We therefore pool the two values and calculate s on the basis of:

$$s^2 = \frac{n_1 s_1^2 + n_2 s_2^2}{(n_1 - 1) + (n_2 - 1)}$$

This ought to look familiar to you as the weighted average of the two sample variances although we are using degrees of freedom on the bottom line as the divisor. Some writers suggest using the degrees of freedom as the weights. That has a certain symmetry to it and if you wanted to you could calculate:

$$s^2 = \frac{(n_1 - 1) s_1^2 + (n_2 - 1) s_2^2}{(n_1 - 1) + (n_2 - 1)}$$

This makes for a little more arithmetic but may be easier to remember. We'll use this second form in our examples.

We might also note that, when performing hypotheses tests of this kind, the number of degrees of freedom is given by the sum of the two individual values, i.e.:

$$\text{d.f.} = (n_1 - 1) + (n_2 - 1)$$

Let's look at an example.

Samples of bags of cement produced in a manufacturing plant are taken on two consecutive days and checked for weight. On the first day the average weight of the 9 bags tested was 50.2 kg with a sample standard deviation of 0.2 kg. On day two the 11 bags tested weighed on average 49.9 kg with a sample standard deviation of 0.1 kg. Is there any evidence to suggest that the machine being used to fill the bags should be checked to ensure that the settings have not been changed?

Note first of all that the way in which the question is framed suggests that we are effectively dealing with two populations with equal variances. The first sample was taken from the population of bags filled on day one and the second from the population of bags filled on day two. It is clearly the intention that the two populations have the same variance and so we may assume this to be the case.

First of all let's calculate s. We have:

$$s^2 = \frac{(n_1 - 1)s_1^2 + (n_2 - 1)s_2^2}{(n_1 - 1) + (n_2 - 1)}$$

$$= \frac{(9 - 1)0.2^2 + (11 - 1)0.1^2}{(9 - 1) + (11 - 1)}$$

$$= \frac{0.32 + 0.10}{18}$$

$$= 0.0233$$

and therefore $s = 0.1526$.

Now we can calculate the value of the test statistic t. As usual we'll work at the 5% level of significance:

$$t = \frac{(\overline{x}_1 - \overline{x}_2) - D_0}{s\sqrt{\dfrac{1}{n_1} + \dfrac{1}{n_2}}}$$

$$= \frac{(50.2 - 49.9) - 0}{0.1526\sqrt{\dfrac{1}{9} + \dfrac{1}{11}}}$$

$$= \frac{0.3}{0.0685}$$

$$= 4.38$$

We've been a bit sloppy up to now since we haven't set out the null hypothesis and the alternative hypothesis, and so we really ought to do that now. We are presumably concerned to detect bags that are both underweight and overweight, which implies that we want to do a two-tailed test. That means therefore that we want to divide the significance between the two tails, i.e. put 2.5% in each. Our hypotheses are therefore formally stated as:

$H_0 : \mu_1 - \mu_2 = 0$

$H_a : \mu_1 - \mu_2 \neq 0$

Crucial tip	It may seem tiresome to have to set out the hypotheses formally. However, you should always do so since it may be that some credit will be given even if you don't get the rest of the calculation correct.

and the critical value of the test statistic, with 18 d.f., is 2.101. Our calculated value of 4.38 is much greater than this and therefore we may reject the null hypothesis quite confidently. It appears that we should investigate the setting on our bag filling machine.

Quick test

1. Under what circumstances should we use the *t*-distribution?

2. In what way does knowledge of the values of the *t*-distribution help to explain why many statisticians would regard a sample of 30 or more as 'large'?

3. What additional factor needs to be taken into account when conducting a *t*-test?

Crucial examples

1. Dietary guidelines for the production of patients' meals in hospitals suggest that adherence to the guidelines should lead to an average daily expenditure of £2.65 per meal and that this should be normally distributed with a standard deviation of 13p. The Anywhere Hospital Trust undertakes an investigation into its own catering expenditure and discovers that it is spending, on average, £2.29 on its meals. Is there evidence, at the 99% level, to suggest that the Trust may not be complying with national guidelines?

2. What kinds of errors may you make when carrying out an hypothesis test?

Answers

1. There are two ways in which the Trust might depart from national guidelines: it might spend more than it should on food or it might spend less. This therefore suggests to us that we are looking to carry out a two-tailed test. Our informal hypothesis is that the average we have obtained from the Trust's records is consistent with what we would have got if we had taken a random sample from the population of hospitals on which the national guidelines are based. What we really want to know therefore is whether or not it is likely that the actual value obtained, £2.29, could have come from the national population. Note that in this example we know the population standard deviation and therefore use a slightly different version of the formula for the test statistic. We follow the drill:

State the null hypothesis $H_o : \mu = 2.65$

State the alternative hypothesis $H_a : \mu \neq 2.65$

Calculate the value of the test statistic
$$z = \frac{\bar{x} - \mu}{\sigma}$$
$$= \frac{2.29 - 2.65}{0.13}$$
$$= -2.77$$

Determine the rejection region   Here we will set $\alpha = 0.01$. Because this is a two-tailed test the rejection region will be spread over both tails and so we want to calculate the critical value that results in 0.005 in each tail. From tables this is 2.58. We will therefore reject the null hypothesis if our calculated value is less than −2.58 or greater than +2.58.

Decide   The calculated value of our test statistic at −2.77 is less than the critical value of −2.58 and so we reject the null hypothesis.

It seems that they are not complying with national guidelines.

2. In carrying out a hypothesis test you may make one (but not both) of the following kinds of error:

   • You might reject the null hypothesis when really it is true. This kind of error is called a Type I error. Its size is controllable by selecting an appropriate α value.

   • You might fail to reject the null hypothesis when it is false. This is known as a Type II error. In general terms its size depends on how close the hypothesised values and the actual value really are, and is often more difficult to determine and hence to fix in advance.

Crucial reading and research

Reading
Curwin, J. and Slater, R. (2002) *Quantitative Methods for Business Decision*, 5th edn. Thomson Learning. See Chapter 12: Significance Testing (pp. 275–97) and Chapter 13: Non-Parametric Tests (pp. 301–15).

Lewis, J.P. and Trail, A. (1999) *Statistics Explained*, Addison-Wesley. See Chapters 25–7 and 29.

Lucey, T. (1996) *Quantitative Techniques*, 5th edn. Letts Educational. See Chapter 6: Statistics – Hypothesis Testing (pp. 82–101).

Mendenhall, W., Reinmuth, J.E. and Beaver, R.J., (1993) *Statistics for Management and Economics*, 7th edn. Duxbury Press. See Chapters 9 and 10.

Philips, J.L. Jr (1999) *How to Think about Statistics,* revised edition. W.H. Freeman. See Chapters 7 and 8.

Research
We've tried to adopt a deliberately straightforward approach to the subject of hypothesis testing. However, you ought to be aware that real life can throw up a number of complications that can make the application of these techniques rather more involved than we have suggested here. The reading references all contain a good deal of advanced reading that will help you to develop your knowledge and understanding, as well as further references.

The tests described in this chapter have been of means or proportions. However, the principles of hypothesis testing can be applied to other tests, including those designed to indicate whether observed differences between **variances** are significant. You might want to pursue this area: again the texts referred to above will give you a more than adequate grounding.

CORRELATION
AND REGRESSION

Chapter summary

A common problem in business is to determine the extent to which there appears to be a relationship between two or more variables and, if so, to quantify the strength of that relationship. A related problem is to predict or forecast the value of some variable in the future given knowledge of the value of another variable to which it is related. Problems of this kind are often suitable for solving using the techniques of **correlation**, to determine the nature and strength of the relationship between two variables, and **regression**, to make the forecast. This chapter describes how to perform the calculations necessary to measure correlation and to perform regression in simple cases.

This chapter also deals with another important topic in inferential statistics, testing whether or not there is an association between two variables. We will concentrate on one very specific non-parametric test of this kind – the chi-square test.

Studying this chapter will help you to:

- determine the nature and strength of the relationship between two variables;
- make estimates of the future values of variables based on the relationship between them;
- test whether the value of one variable is contingent upon the value of another.

Assessment targets

Target 1

Calculate the Pearson product-moment coefficient of correlation and the coefficient of determination. This is tested in Question 1 at the end of this chapter.

Target 2

Calculate the least squares regression line of a single dependent variable on the independent variable. See Question 2 at the end of this chapter for this.

Target 3

Perform a chi-square test. Use Question 3 at the end of this chapter to test this.

Crucial concepts

These are the key terms and concepts you will meet in this chapter:

Chi-square	Degrees of freedom
Coefficient of determination	Least squares regression
Contingency table	Product-moment coefficient of correlation

Relevant links

The material in this chapter is relatively self-contained.

Section 1	Correlation: the product-moment coefficient

What are you studying?

This section describes the concept of correlation between two variables and explains how to calculate the most common measure of correlation known as the **Pearson product-moment coefficient of correlation**.

How will you be assessed on this?

You may be asked to calculate the Pearson product-moment coefficient of correlation given a data set. Once calculated you may be asked to comment on your findings and discuss any limitations on the calculation that may exist.

It is quite common in business settings to want to determine the nature of the relationship between two variables. This is often done by measuring what is known as the **Pearson product-moment coefficient of correlation** and we'll illustrate its calculation with an example.

> Crucial concept The **Pearson product-moment coefficient of correlation** measures the strength of the relationship between two variables.

Imagine a company whose monthly sales income and advertising expenditure are as follows:

Month	Advertising £000	Sales £000
1	1.20	101
2	0.80	92
3	1.00	110
4	1.30	120
5	0.70	90
6	0.80	82
7	1.00	93
8	0.60	75
9	0.90	91
10	1.10	105

The sales director of the company believes that spending on advertising is associated with changes in sales income has not been able to quantify that. As a first step they decide to plot the two data series on a scattergraph, with the result shown in Figure 6.1.

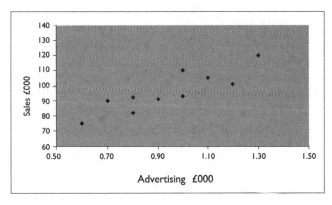

Figure 6.1   Scattergraph of data series

From the chart it appears that there is some relationship between the two variables: as spending on advertising (on the x-axis) increases then so also does sales income. This kind of pattern is an indication that the two variables are **correlated**. To measure the strength of that correlation we need to calculate the **Pearson product-moment coefficient of correlation**, denoted by r:

$$r = \frac{S_{xy}}{\sqrt{S_{xx} S_{yy}}}$$

where:

$$S_{xy} = \sum_i (x_i - \bar{x})^2 (y_i - \bar{y})^2$$

$$S_{xx} = \sum_i (x_i - \bar{x})^2$$

$$S_{yy} = \sum_i (y_i - \bar{y})^2$$

These formulae are the correct 'theoretical' ones for the product-moment coefficient of correlation. However, it turns out that if we rearrange them a bit we can get the same answer with fewer sums. As a side benefit this will also help us with the calculations that we need to do later in this chapter when we come to talk about regression. So, the rearranged expressions that we'll actually use to do our sums are:

$$S_{xy} = \sum_i x_i y_i - \frac{\left(\sum_i x_i\right)\left(\sum_i y_i\right)}{n}$$

$$S_{xx} = \sum_i x_i^2 - \frac{\left(\sum_i x_i\right)^2}{n}$$

$$S_{yy} = \sum_i y_i^2 - \frac{\left(\sum_i y_i\right)^2}{n}$$

> **Crucial tip**   The second set of formulae shown here reduces the amount of computation that you will have to do to calculate the Pearson product-moment coefficient of correlation. You should use these to minimise the amount of work to be done and also the possibility of error.

Rather than talk about this let's see how we work it out using the real data:

$$S_{xy} = \sum_i x_i y_i - \frac{\left(\sum_i x_i\right)\left(\sum_i y_i\right)}{n}$$
$$= 924.80 - \frac{9.40 \times 959}{10}$$
$$= 924.80 - 901.46$$
$$= 23.34$$

$$S_{xx} = \sum_i x_i^2 - \frac{\left(\sum_i x_i\right)^2}{n}$$
$$= 9.28 - \frac{9.40^2}{10}$$
$$= 9.28 - 8.836$$
$$= 0.444$$

$$S_{yy} = \sum_i y_i^2 - \frac{\left(\sum_i y_i\right)^2}{n}$$
$$= 93,569 - \frac{959^2}{10}$$
$$= 93,569 - 91,968.1$$
$$= 1,600.9$$

$$r = \frac{S_{xy}}{\sqrt{S_{xx}S_{yy}}}$$
$$= \frac{23.34}{\sqrt{0.444 \times 1,600.9}}$$
$$= \frac{23.34}{26.66}$$
$$= 0.88$$

We have calculated that the Pearson product-moment coefficient of correlation for our data is 0.88. What does that mean?

To answer that we need to know some things about this correlation coefficient:

- It can only take on values between −1 and +1.
- If two sets of data have a correlation coefficient of −1 exactly then we say that they are **perfectly negatively correlated**.
- If the coefficient is +1 then we say that the data is **perfectly positively correlated**.
- A value of 0 means that the two data sets are not correlated at all – there is no relationship between the two data sets, which are therefore independent.

Crucial concept The **Pearson product-moment coefficient of correlation** can take values between −1 and +1 only. The closer the coefficient is to ±1 the more perfectly correlated the two variables are. A coefficient of 0 means there is no correlation between the two sets of data.

Our value was 0.88. You might reasonably ask if that shows a strong relationship between the two sets of data. Most statisticians would probably agree that it does, although to understand why that is so we need to know about another statistic that is very closely related to the coefficient of correlation – the **coefficient of determination**. This is a very easy statistic to calculate, and one that perhaps gives us more information than the coefficient of correlation. We calculate it by simply squaring r and therefore we usually denote it by r^2. So, for our calculated value of r of 0.88 we get a value of r^2 of 0.774 The coefficient of determination measures how much of the variance in the y values is explained by the variance in the x values. In our case variance in advertising expenditure accounts for just over 77% of the variance in sales income.

Crucial concept The **coefficient of determination** (r^2) measures the proportion of variance in the y variable that is explained by variance in the x variable. It takes values between 0 and 1 and is simply calculated as the square of r.

Crucial tip An r of much less than about 0.7 indicates a relatively weak relationship. This is because the coefficient of determination for such an r is only 0.49, indicating that less than half of the variance is being explained.

Quick test

1. What range of values can the Pearson product-moment coefficient take on?
2. What is the relationship between the coefficient of determination and the coefficient of correlation?
3. What does the Pearson product-moment coefficient of correlation measure?
4. Two variables have a correlation coefficient of 0.65. Does that indicate strong correlation between them?
5. Explain why the coefficient of determination can take on values only between 0 and 1.
6. If two variables are perfectly positively correlated does that show that one is caused by the other?

Chapter 6 • Correlation and regression

97

Section 2   Regression

What are you studying?
This section describes how to use simple regression to make predictions about the value of one variable given knowledge of the value of another to which it is related.

How will you be assessed on this?
You may be asked to calculate and plot the least squares regression line given a set of data points. This might be assessed in the context of also being asked to calculate the Pearson product-moment coefficient of correlation.

As well as being asked to calculate the regression line you may also be asked to interpret it and/ or explain its meaning. Once calculated you may be asked to predict values of the dependent variable given values of the independent variable.

Let's go back to our company from the first section and consider again their sales and advertising figures:

Month	Advertising £000	Sales £000
1	1.20	101
2	0.80	92
3	1.00	110
4	1.30	120
5	0.70	90
6	0.80	82
7	1.00	93
8	0.60	75
9	0.90	91
10	1.10	105

The sales director is interested in knowing whether they can predict future sales income given a plan to spend a fixed a amount on advertising.

From the newly acquired knowledge of the Pearson product-moment coefficient of correlation they know that the two variables are quite strongly correlated. But how can they use this data to predict future levels of sales income based on planned expenditure on advertising? The answer is to use a formula to calculate the coefficients of a straight line that will provide a best fit to the given data points (see Figure 6.2). The line that results is called the **least squares regression** line.

> Crucial concept The **least squares regression** line is the line that minimises the sum of the squared deviations of each point from the line. In a linear regression problem it is the line of best fit.

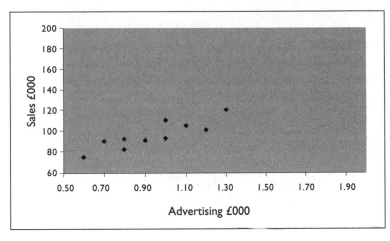

Figure 6.2   Scattergraph of data series

The least squares regression line of *y* on *x* is given by the formula:

$y = a + bx$ where

$$a = \frac{\sum y \sum x^2 - \sum x \sum xy}{n \sum x^2 - \left(\sum x\right)^2}$$

$$b = \frac{n \sum xy - \sum x \sum y}{n \sum x^2 - \left(\sum x\right)^2}$$

> **Crucial tip**   When using the formulae to calculate a and b you only need to work out the bottom line once.

Let's do that with our sales and advertising data.

Month	x	y	x^2	xy
1	1.20	101	1.44	121.20
2	0.80	92	0.64	73.60
3	1.00	110	1.00	110.00
4	1.30	120	1.69	156.00
5	0.70	90	0.49	63.00
6	0.80	82	0.64	65.60
7	1.00	93	1.00	93.00
8	0.60	75	0.36	45.00
9	0.90	91	0.81	81.90
10	1.10	105	1.21	115.50
$\sum x$	9.40			
$\sum y$		959		
$\sum x^2$			9.28	
$\sum xy$				924.80
$\left(\sum x\right)^2$	88.36			

and so:

$$a = \frac{959 \times 9.28 - 9.4 \times 924.8}{10 \times 9.28 - 88.36}$$

$$= \frac{8899.52 - 8693.12}{92.8 - 88.36}$$

$$= \frac{206.4}{4.44}$$

$$= 46.49$$

$$b = \frac{10 \times 924.8 - 9.4 \times 959}{4.44}$$

$$= \frac{9248 - 9014.6}{4.44}$$

$$= \frac{233.4}{4.44}$$

$$= 52.57$$

We can write the least squares regression line as:

$$y = 46.49 + 52.57x$$

This tells us that if we spend an extra £1,000 on advertising then we should expect to see an increase in sales revenue of over £50,000 (£52,570 to be precise). That's the meaning of the b-value, which is known as the **coefficient** of x. The other thing that this equation lets us do is predict how much sales income will arise from any given level of advertising expenditure. For example, if we spend £1,400 in any month on advertising then we ought to see that generate sales income of just over £120,000. So we can use the output from our regression analysis to make predictions about the future as well as to analyse the relationship between business variables.

Crucial tip	Beware of assuming a causal relationship between two variables in a regression analysis. If there is a relationship it may be based on some other variable or factor that you have not identified.

Another caveat when dealing with regression is that, strictly speaking, the results only hold good for the range within which the original data lie. In our sales and advertising example advertising expenditure ranged from 0.6 to 1.3. If we wanted to say something about sales from expenditure of 2.0 then it may be that the relationship would be different at that point.

When we talk about two variables in regression analysis we often refer to one as the **independent** variable and the other as the **dependent** variable. In this example spending on advertising was the independent variable (the one that we would wish to change) and sales revenue the dependent one (the one whose resulting value we want to estimate). When we treat the variables this way round we say we are calculating the least squares regression line of **y on x**. If we had done things the other way round and treated y as the independent variable then we would have calculated the least squares regression line of x on y. **You should be aware that in general terms the equations produced by each type of regression would be different**. In practice you would normally choose to arrange the variables so that x was the independent one and y the dependent one.

Crucial concept	The variable whose value we feel free to change is called the **independent** variable. The one whose value we expect to change as a result is the **dependent** variable.

We are usually free to choose which variable we call x and which we call y. There will usually be a 'natural' way to do this and you should usually work with x as the independent variable and y as the dependent one.

Do a quick plot of the pairs of x- and y-values to establish whether you expect the slope of the line to be positive (sloping up from left to right) or negative (sloping downwards from left to right). Use that to double check the sign of the x-coefficient in the regression formula.

Check your regression equation by substituting the mean of the x-values into the regression equation. If you don't get the mean of the y-values as a result then you've made a mistake.

You need to be particularly careful in attributing meaning to the value of the *a* coefficient, the point where the line cuts the y-axis. In our sales and advertising example this was 46.49. Because x is 0 at the point where the line cuts the y-axis this implies that spending nothing on advertising would result in sales income of nearly £50,000. This may well be the case but it might equally well not be so.

In the section on correlation we said that the 'alternative' formula used to calculate the Pearson product-moment coefficient of correlation could be helpful in calculating the regression line. In fact there is an alternative formulation of the regression formulae that is easier to use if you are being asked to calculate both the correlation coefficient (and/or the coefficient of determination) and plot the regression line. This alternative version for regression is:

$$y = a + bx$$
$$b = \frac{S_{xy}}{S_{xx}}$$
$$a = \bar{y} - b\bar{x}$$

The terms involved in calculating *b* have all been worked out for the Pearson calculation and the work that remains to be done to calculate *a* is almost trivial.

If you are asked to calculate both the Pearson product-moment coefficient of correlation and the regression line then use the alternative formulation of the regression line shown above to drastically reduce your workload.

From the work we did in the section on correlation we calculated that S_{xy} was 23.34 and S_{xx} was 0.444 so this immediately gives 52.57 for *b*. We calculate $\bar{x}$ and $\bar{y}$ to be 0.94 and 95.90 respectively, which therefore gives 46.48 for *a* (the minor difference from the value calculated previously is due to rounding). If we had already had to work out Pearson then this would have been a much quicker way to calculate the coefficients of the regression equation.

Quick test

1. What are the main constraints on using the output of the regression equation?
2. Interpret the meaning of the two regression coefficients a and b.
3. If two data sets show positive correlation would you expect the regression line to slope up from left to right or down?

Section 3 — Contingency tables and the chi-square test

What are you studying?

This section introduces the idea of a contingency table and sets out the basic steps to follow in performing a chi-square test.

How will you be assessed on this?

You may be asked to perform a chi-square test and explain or interpret the results.

Probably the simplest way to introduce the idea of a contingency table is to start with an example.

The Housing Department of Anywhere Council has produced a leaflet explaining tenants' entitlement to housing benefit. The design team have printed trial versions of the leaflet in three different layouts, each with different costs to produce. They wish to establish whether tenants are likely to choose one leaflet over the others. From trials with leaflets placed at various locations it is established that 23 people preferred leaflet A, 36 leaflet B and 31 leaflet C. Advise the leader of the design team on whether there is any evidence that tenants have a preference for one leaflet over the others.

The first thing to notice about this example is that the data is presented in the form of frequencies or counts – the number of people choosing each type of leaflet. Problems involving chi-square tests are always of this kind. The second point to make is that the general approach that we have used in our previous work on estimating and hypothesis testing can't be used here. The essence of our approach will be to determine what we would expect our data to be if there were no association between the data items. Then, based on those expected values, we'll calculate the value of a test statistic called chi-square, and use that to determine whether or not we may reject the null hypothesis of no association. Let's get started and see how we go about this.

We'll set out our data in the form of a table. Let's start with what we know:

	Observed frequency
Leaflet A	23
Leaflet B	36
Leaflet C	31

The next thing we do is augment the table by working out what we would expect to find if there were no association between the leaflet design and preference. If that were the case. i.e. if people really were indifferent as to which leaflet they preferred, then we might reasonably have expected to find equal preferences. We have 90 responses in total and so might have expected to get 30 people preferring each one. We'll add that data to the table:

	Observed frequency	Expected frequency
Leaflet A	23	30
Leaflet B	36	30
Leaflet C	31	30

Now for the arithmetic. We will calculate the value of our test statistic, chi-square.

Crucial concept	The sum of the result of dividing the square of the differences between the observed values and expected values is called the **chi-square** statistic. It can be shown that in repeated sampling it has a chi-square probability distribution.

It's easier to do than to say so let's do it:

	Observed frequency	Expected frequency	$O-E^2$	$(O-E)^2/E$
Leaflet A	23	30	49	1.633
Leaflet B	36	30	36	1.200
Leaflet C	31	30	1	0.033
Sum				2.866

At this point in a 'normal' hypothesis test we would expect to look up some critical value of our test statistic and determine whether our calculated value is greater than it or not. We do just that here. However, we need to use a different table, a table of chi-square values, and we need to introduce again the idea of degrees of freedom. If you have worked through the material on testing hypotheses based on small samples then you may remember this. It is complex to explain the reasoning behind the concept of degrees of freedom so we'll content ourselves with simply learning how to calculate it and apply it. In this simple case, we look at our original data and work out one less than the number of data items. Here we have three and so there are 2 degrees of freedom.

Crucial concept	The number of **degrees of freedom** measures the number of row and column frequencies that we are free to vary without altering the row and column totals

Here's an extract from the chi-square (sometimes referred to as χ^2, using the Greek notation) table that shows the area in the upper tail of the distribution for the 5%, 2.5% and 1% significance levels, for selected degrees of freedom.

$\alpha =$	0.05	0.025	0.01
$v = 1$	3.841	5.024	6.635
2	5.991	7.378	9.210
3	7.815	9.348	11.345
4	9.488	11.143	13.277
5	11.070	12.832	15.086

To use the table you locate the intersection of the significance level that you are interested in and the degrees of freedom of the data. Here we have 2 d.f. and we will use the 5% (0.05) significance level. The value of chi-square is 5.991 and this is therefore the critical value of our test statistic in this example. Since our calculated value of 2.866 is less than this critical value we have no reason to reject the null hypothesis, that there is an association between leaflet type and consumer preference.

Crucial tip	Be sure to take into account the correct number of degrees of freedom associated with your data when looking up a chi-square value from tables.

We've looked at an example of the simplest kind of chi-square test, involving one variable. Let's look at a slightly more involved example that has two variables.

The Newtown Council has recently built a new library, complete with state-of-the-art systems for providing Internet and multimedia information to users. The Director of Leisure and Recreation wishes to know whether there is any difference in usage of the new facility when compared with the more traditional library. They collect the usage information shown below and asks you to advise whether the new facility is attracting a different age group.

Age range	New facility	Traditional library
7 – 11	27	14
12 – 18	54	29
Over 18	35	41

Note that once again we have set out our data in the form of a table. We call tables of this kind **contingency tables**.

Crucial concept	A contingency table is a two-way classification of data into r rows and c columns. The name comes from the fact that we are hypothesising that one set of data depends on or is **contingent** upon the other.

We take the same broad approach to this one as we did to the first example. However, you will find that calculating the expected frequencies is a little more complicated due to the addition of the second variable. We'll set out our data in a way that should help you to see how we go about this.

Age range	New facility	Traditional library	Totals
7 – 11	A	B	41
12 – 18	C	D	83
Over 18	E	F	76
	116	84	200

In this second table we have set out only the row and column totals, based on the data in the first table. We will use this to fill in our expected data, using what we know about the totals and assuming that there is no association between age range and preference for type of library. We can take each cell in turn and work out the expected value based on the totals. Let's take the first blank cell (the one labelled 'A') and work it through as an example. Now we know that 116 out of 200 people preferred the new facility to the more traditional one. If there is no association between age range and preference then we would expect the same proportion in each age group to prefer the new facility. So, taking cell A to start with, if 116/200 in total preferred the new facility then we would expect to find 116/200 x 41 of the 7–11 age range expressing a preference for it, i.e. 23.78. So A is 23.78. Note that you should generally work with decimal fractions at this stage.

Working through the rest of the cells in the same way gives us our table of expected values:

Age range	New facility	Traditional library	Total
7 – 11	A = 23.78	B = 17.22	41
12 – 18	C = 48.14	D = 34.86	83
Over 18	E = 44.08	F = 31.92	76
	116	84	200

> **Crucial tip**   The row and column sums in a contingency table are fixed. When you calculate the cell values make sure that they add to the row and column totals. If not then you have made an error in your calculations.

We can now calculate the difference between the observed and expected values and proceed with the calculation of chi-square as we did in the first example.

	Observed frequency	Expected frequency	$O–E^2$	$(O–E)^2/E$
A	27	23.78	10.3684	0.4360
B	14	17.22	10.3684	0.6021
C	54	48.14	34.3396	0.7133
D	29	34.86	34.3396	0.9851
E	35	44.08	82.4464	1.8703
F	41	31.92	82.4464	2.5829
Sum				7.1897

The calculated value of the test statistic is 7.1897. Now we need to determine the critical value. We need to know the significance level, which we'll take as 5% again, and the number of degrees of freedom. For a two-way contingency table, which we have here, the number of degrees of freedom is given by the number of rows (excluding titles and totals) less 1 times the number of columns (again less titles and totals) less 1.

> **Crucial tip**   In a two-way contingency table the number of degrees of freedom is equal to the product of the number of rows less one and the number of columns less one. In both cases ignore rows and columns that contain totals, labels and anything other than raw data.

Here we have three rows containing 'real' data and two columns so we have $(3 − 1) \times (2 − 1) = 2$ degrees of freedom. The critical value of the chi-square statistic at the 5% level with 2 d.f. is 5.991 as we saw in the first example. Our calculated value is greater than this and so we may reject the null hypothesis. It appears that there is some association between age range and preference for type of library. Note that this does not tell us anything about the strength of the association, although it is reasonable to assume from inspecting the data that the new facility is preferred by all age groups.

For the chi-square test to be appropriate it is necessary that all of the expected cell values be greater than 5. If you find that this is not the case then the safest thing to do is to combine cells until that is so. The procedure for doing this is not particularly complex and you may follow it up in the research and readings references for this chapter.

Quick test

1. Where is the rejection region in the chi-square distribution?
2. How many degrees of freedom will there be in a 5 x 4 contingency table?

Crucial examples

1. Calculate the Pearson product-moment coefficient of correlation and the coefficient of determination for the following data set:

x	y
23.2	33.4
45.8	75.2
52.5	75.2
66.4	79.8
17.6	54.6
18.2	23.5
16.5	55.0
66.4	95.5
8.3	47.7

2. Using the data set from Question 1 determine the least squares regression line of y on x and estimate the y-value that would result given an x-value of 60.
3. A survey of shoppers found the following association between socio-economic grouping and preferences for shopping:

| Observed | Shopping preference | |
Socio-economic group	Local	Out of town
A	38	22
B	62	58
C	30	41

Is there any evidence, at the 95% level of confidence, to believe that there is an association between socio-economic grouping and shopping preference?

Answers

1. We use the 'quick' version of the formulae and set out our data in tabular fashion

	x	y	xy	x^2	y
	23.20	33.40	774.88	538.24	1,115.56
	45.80	75.20	3,444.16	2,097.64	5,655.04
	52.50	75.20	3,948.00	2,756.25	5,655.04
	66.40	79.80	5,298.72	4,408.96	6,368.04
	17.60	54.60	960.96	309.76	2,981.16
	18.20	23.50	427.70	331.24	552.25
	16.50	55.00	907.50	272.25	3,025.00
	66.40	95.50	6,341.20	4,408.96	9,120.25
	8.30	47.70	395.91	68.89	2,275.29
Σ	314.90	539.90	22,499.03	15,192.19	36,747.63

Substituting these values into the formula gives:

$$S_{xy} = \sum_i x_i y_i - \frac{\left(\sum_i x_i\right)\left(\sum_i y_i\right)}{n}$$

$$= 22,499.03 - \frac{314.90 \times 539.90}{9}$$

$$= 22,499.03 - 18,890.50$$

$$= 3,608.53$$

$$S_{xx} = \sum_i x_i^2 - \frac{\left(\sum_i x_i\right)^2}{n}$$

$$= 15,192.19 - \frac{314.90^2}{9}$$

$$= 15,192.19 - 11,018.00$$

$$= 4,174.19$$

$$S_{yy} = \sum_i y_i^2 - \frac{\left(\sum_i y_i\right)^2}{n}$$

$$= 36,747.63 - \frac{539.90^2}{9}$$

$$= 36,747.63 - 32,388.00$$

$$= 4,359.63$$

$$r = \frac{S_{xy}}{\sqrt{S_{xx}S_{yy}}}$$

$$= \frac{3,608.53}{\sqrt{4,174.19 \times 4,359.63}}$$

$$= \frac{3,608.53}{4,265.90}$$

$$= 0.8459$$

The coefficient of determination is therefore 0.7155.

2. Having done most of the work in the first question the calculation of the coefficients for the linear regression line is quite straightforward:

$$y = a + bx$$

$$b = \frac{S_{xy}}{S_{xx}}$$

$$a = \bar{y} - b\bar{x}$$

so $b = 0.8645$ and $a = 59.99 - 0.8645 \times 34.99 = 29.7411$

Therefore $y = 20.74 + 0.86x$ and if x is 60 then y will be 81.34.

3. We tabulate our results and calculate the value of the chi-squared statistic:

Observed Socio-economic group	Shopping preference Local	Out of town	Total
A	38	22	60
B	62	58	120
C	30	41	71
	130	121	251

Expected Socio-economic group	Shopping preference Local	Out of town	Total
A	31.0757	28.9243	60.0000
B	62.1514	57.8486	120.0000
C	36.7729	34.2271	71.0000
130.0000	121.0000	251.0000	

Degrees of freedom   2

Critical value of the chi-square
statistic at 95% with 2 d.f.   5.991

$$\chi^2 = \sum \frac{(O - E)^2}{E}$$

O	E	$(O - E)^2$	$(O - E)^2/E$
38	31.0757	47.94593	1.543
62	62.1514	0.022922	0.000
30	36.7729	45.87217	1.247
22	28.9243	47.94593	1.658
58	57.8486	0.022922	0.000
41	34.2271	45.87217	1.340
			5.789

The calculated value is less than the critical value and so we have no basis to reject the null hypothesis of no association. Note, however, that the difference between the critical value and the calculated value is quite small and therefore we might wish to consider some additional research into this area.

Crucial reading and research

Reading

Curwin, J. and Slater, R. (2002) *Quantitative Methods for Business Decisions*, 5th edn. Thomson Learning. See Chapter 15: Correlation (pp. 365–82) and Chapter 16: Regression (pp. 390–402).

Lewis, J.P. and Trail, A. (1999) *Statistics Explained*, Addison-Wesley. Chapters 14, 31 and 36.

Lucey, T. (1996) *Quantitative Techniques*, 5th edn. Letts Educational. See Chapter 7: Correlation and Regression (pp. 109–26).

Mendenhall, W., Reinmuth, J.E. and Beaver, R.J. (1993) *Statistics for Management and Economics*, 7th edn. Duxbury Press. See Chapter 12.

Philips, J.L. Jr. (1999) *How to Think about Statistics,* revised edn. W.H. Freeman. See Chapters 9 and 10.

Research

This chapter has concentrated on the most basic application of regression: linear regression involving a single independent variable. However, in real life you will find that relationships are often more complex than this. To explain the behaviour of a single dependent variable often requires knowledge of its relationship with a number of independent variables. In addition the nature of the relationship is often more complex than simply linear. The technique of **multiple regression** is used to describe such relationships: if you are interested in how it works then Chapter 13 in Mendenhall *et al.* would make a good starting point.

CHAPTER 7

FORECASTING TECHNIQUES

Chapter summary

A significant part of a manager's decision-making is related to the future, and so there is a need to have some way of predicting, estimating or guessing what will occur in the future. In this chapter we will be looking at different techniques that help decision-makers to take the available information and process it in a systematic way, thereby gaining some assistance in making decisions about the future.

This chapter will help you to:

- apply the high-low method of forecasting;
- use the time series model to identify trends and other components;
- apply exponential smoothing to make forecasts;
- relate the topic of forecasting to the linear regression technique (Chapter 6).

Assessment targets

Target 1
The high-low method is a very simple technique. It is possible to be asked to use this technique alongside others (e.g. linear regression) and critically appraise the results. Question 1 at the end of this chapter assesses this.

Target 2
You need to know how to calculate a moving average. Question 2 at the end of this chapter gives a test to see whether you have grasped this.

Target 3
An examination question can ask you to take raw data, summarise it for ease of analysis, and use time series analysis to identify the main components of the series. Question 3 at the end of this chapter tests you on this topic.

Target 4
Exponential smoothing is a fairly straightforward technique. You would be expected to be able to apply the basic formula to a range of results to determine a forecast, and also to explain the use of the technique. Question 4 at the end of this chapter tests the application of this technique.

Crucial concepts

These are the key terms and concepts you will meet in this chapter:

Additive model	Projection
Exponential smoothing	Qualitative techniques
Forecasting	Quantitative techniques
High-low method	Seasonally adjusted figures
Moving averages	Time series
Prediction	

Relevant links

Time series analysis and exponential smoothing are self-contained topics, but the general subject of forecasting is closely related to linear regression. As discussed in Chapter 6, linear regression can be used to obtain a 'line of best fit', and this line can be used to forecast future outcomes, provided that the two items being compared are correlated.

Section 1   Forecasting

What are you studying?
In this chapter we will look at different techniques that help managers make forecasts. It is important to see these techniques in the context of real-life situations. In this section we will

look briefly at how forecasting is used in situations such as planning in manufacturing companies, assessing demand for public services, understanding market trends, etc.

How will you be assessed on this?

As well as calculating figures, it is common for assessments to look for some appreciation of the ways in which results should (and should not) be applied in real situations. This sometimes appears as a small section at the end of a numerical question (e.g. 5 marks out of 25), but for many students this can make a real impact on their overall chances of passing.

Crucial tip	Always make an attempt at small narrative questions tagged on to the end of numerical questions. The marks are often easier to obtain than in the numerical part, but it is essential to make separate and specific points in your answer – avoid waffling! If there are five marks available, try and make five clear and relevant statements.

One question that is worth considering is 'what exactly do we mean by forecasting'? In other words, if a manager wishes to make a forecast, what status does it have? Does it mean what is most likely to happen, what will happen if the circumstances don't change, an average of all possible outcomes, etc.? Some texts will make a distinction in this area between the terms 'projection', 'forecasting' and 'prediction'.

Crucial concepts	**Projection** is a mechanistic approach that involves the use of historical data and extending this information into the future. **Prediction** adds the influence of external factors, and is therefore more realistic than projection. And **forecasting** takes this further by adding the judgement of the decision-maker into the model.

In some problems (including examination questions), the numerical data can provide the basis for making a projection. It is usually necessary to extend this analysis to show how external factors (e.g. new legislation or increased competition) would affect the results. And in the real world, the more capable decision-makers use judgement, experience, etc. to determine what final action to take.

A further distinction in forecasting is between techniques that are based on qualitative analysis and those that are quantitative in nature. As the title of this textbook would suggest, our attention will be on quantitative techniques in this chapter. However, you should be aware of the existence of other useful approaches that do not rely on numbers.

Crucial concept	**Qualitative techniques** to forecasting use non-numerical data along with judgement and experience to formulate a decision. **Quantitative techniques** use relevant numerical data to identify patterns and relationships that can be applied to future situations.

It is important to avoid the trap of assuming that a complex statistical approach will necessarily give the 'right' or 'best' answer to a forecasting problem. We will focus for the remainder of this chapter on quantitative techniques, but you should be aware that these have limitations and are not the only methods available to forecasters.

Quick test

1. Think of a situation where a university would need to make a forecast. What type of data might they use?
2. What is the difference between projection, prediction and forecasting?

Section 2	The high-low method

What are you studying?
In this section we will look at one of the simplest methods of producing forecasts, i.e. the high-low method.

How will you be assessed on this?
You will be expected to be able to be able to use the high-low method to produce a trend line for the data and to use this information to produce forecasts. As the method is fairly crude, assessments that include this topic will often expect a criticism of the approach and the results.

This technique is sometimes used to analyse the relationship between costs and activity levels. It operates on the basis of identifying a line that determines the way total costs are made up of fixed costs (i.e. costs that do not change with activity) and variable costs (i.e. costs that vary directly with the level of activity). The approach is a crude one as it focuses on the extreme values in the data, with the assumption being that the other observations in the series will lie close to this line.

> **Crucial concept** The **high-low method** of forecasting uses the extreme values in a set of historic data (e.g. of costs and activity levels) and analyses the values into fixed and variable elements. These can then be predicted for future activity levels to give forecast totals.

Consider the following table, which gives monthly production figures for a year and the associated costs.

Month	Production	Costs £
Jan	5,000	155,000
Feb	4,000	126,000
Mar	3,500	150,500
Apr	2,500	84,600
May	3,900	124,000
Jun	5,500	170,000
Jul	6,000	186,200
Aug	4,500	137,000
Sep	4,800	140,000
Oct	5,000	155,000
Nov	5,100	161,000
Dec	4,400	130,000

The high-low method reduces this to the extreme values, i.e. the results for the two months with the highest and lowest activity:

	Production	Costs £
Low	2,500	84,600
High	6,000	186,200

We can use this to calculate the variable costs, assuming that the increase in costs between lowest activity and highest activity is due entirely to an increase in variable costs.

Difference in production = 6,000 – 2,500 = 3,500 units
Difference in costs = 186,200 – 84,600 = £101,600
Additional cost per unit = 101,600 / 3,500 = £29.03

And now that we know the variable cost per unit, we can estimate the fixed costs using either of the activity levels, i.e.

186,200 – (6,000 x 29.03) = £12,020
or   84,600 – (2,500 x 29.03) = £12,025 (the small difference arising from rounding variable
cost per unit to the nearest penny)

So how is this related to forecasting? The relevance here is that we can now use this relationship to project the costs for any activity level. If, for example, we expect the next month's production to be 4,200 units, we can apply the following equation line to estimate the costs:

Total cost = Fixed costs + (Variable cost per unit x Units produced)
i.e.   Total cost = 12,020 + (4,200 x 29.03) = £133,946

If we look at this line in relation to all the observed values, as shown in Figure 7.1, we can see that it is a reasonable, but far from perfect, basis for estimating in this example.

If you compare this approach with correlation and regression (covered in Chapter 6), it is easy to see that it has several flaws. As well as focusing on extreme values, which might not be representative, it assumes there is a direct linear relationship between costs and activities. We also have no information beyond the values used, so if an activity level higher than experienced in the past is being costed (e.g. a level of 8,000 units in the previous example), we do not know if the assumed relationship will continue in the same way.

Quick test

1. What is the variable cost per unit, given the following data?

Low   200 units   £550
High   900 units   £1,225

(Answer at the end of this chapter.)

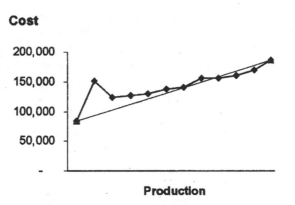

Cost

Figure 7.1 High-low method

What are you studying?

In this section we will introduce the idea of data arranged in a time series and how this can be interpreted through the calculation of moving averages. This topic is taken further in the following section, which looks at the analysis of time series into their component parts.

How will you be assessed on this?

You will be expected to be able to arrange time series information into tabular and chart formats, and also to calculate moving averages from that data. Interpretation of this information is very important, so try and think about what the information means as we work through the topic, as well as the mechanics of applying the technique

Much of the data used by managers in their work is related to time, for example, sales in each quarter for the last five years, expenditure on salary costs each month for the last 12 months, drug costs in a ward on a weekly basis for the last 52 weeks.

Each of these is an example of a time series, and one of the most common uses of such series is to make forecasts of likely future results, given the pattern that has occurred in the past. The past does not determine the future, of course. However, it can often give us some understanding of the relationship between our data series and time, and help us make forecasts about the future.

> Crucial concept   A **time series** is a set of results taken at equal intervals of time. These results can be plotted against time to give an overall picture of the situation.

> Crucial tip   When plotting a time series, you should always show the time data along the horizontal axis.

Time series data often exhibit a general pattern that repeats periodically, or a cycle. Underlying this pattern there may also be a trend, i.e. a consistent movement in a particular direction. In some cases, there may be a seasonal variation, as the results rise and fall over specified intervals of time. We will look at these, and other variations, more closely in the next section.

The moving averages approach is a way of identifying an underlying trend. In a time series involving some fluctuations, this approach averages out the fluctuations (also called 'smoothing') to expose the trend. An example of when this approach could be useful is if one month's figures showed that house prices had risen by a smaller percentage than the previous month. You can probably immediately see that this information on its own is not very useful in terms of indicating whether the trend in house price inflation is increasing, static or decreasing. If that particular month in the year is always sluggish, then a lower percentage increase might be expected. If it is normally a boom month, then this gives a different picture. So we need to put this individual result into a longer set of observations (i.e. a time series) before starting to draw conclusions.

> Crucial concept The **moving averages** technique involves the calculation of the mean of a number of subsets of the time series, based on a knowledge of the underlying period of the series.

Let's look at an example to illustrate how this is done. The table below relates to the number of cheques processed by the finance section of a small company. You should be able to see immediately that there is a pattern, with week 4 of each month being the highest number (perhaps to pay salaries) and week 2 the lowest. For simplicity, we will regard each month as having four weeks.

	Week	Cheques
Jan	1	50
	2	20
	3	25
	4	80
Feb	1	50
	2	25
	3	30
	4	85
Mar	1	50
	2	25
	3	35
	4	100

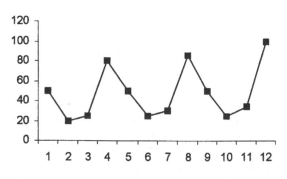

Figure 7.2   Cheques processed January – March

This pattern can be confirmed by plotting the data on a chart as in Figure 7.2.

As well as there being a pattern across the weeks of each month, the figures appear to be increasing over the period from January to March. Calculating a moving averages trend line can tell us whether that is the case or not. The first step in this process is defining the span of the cycle we are observing. The distance in time between successive peaks in the chart is four weeks, so we will calculate moving averages over four periods. This is done by taking the first four observations (as this is a four-weekly cycle) and calculating their average; for example, for weeks January 1 to January 4, the moving average is (50 + 20 + 25 + 80) / 4 = 43.75, and for January 2 to February 1 is (20 + 25 + 80 + 50) / 4 = 43.75. As this is a four-week period, this figure actually relates to the mid point at week 2.5. In order to have figures that relate to weeks January 3 onwards, we need to 'centre' the moving averages. This is done by taking an average of two monthly moving averages; for example, for week January 4 the centred moving average is (43.75 + 45.00) / 2 = 44.38. This step is not necessary if you are dealing with a cycle with an odd number of observations (e.g. five years). We can now add the centred monthly moving average information to our table and chart (see Figure 7.3) to indicate the underlying trend, which shows a slight increase in the number of cheques being processed.

	Week	Cheques	Monthly MA	Centred monthly MA
Jan	1	50		
	2	20		
	3	25	43.75	43.75
	4	80	43.75	44.38
Feb	1	50	45.00	45.63
	2	25	46.25	46.88
	3	30	47.50	47.50
	4	85	47.50	47.50
Mar	1	50	47.50	48.13
	2	25	48.75	
	3	35		
	4	100		

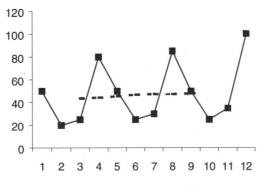

Figure 7.3 Moving averages trend line

We could use this trend to make forecasts, but it would clearly be inaccurate for specific weeks as it does not reflect the four-weekly pattern. Another of the limitations of moving averages is that the technique does not give greater importance to the most recent observations. We will see later in this chapter that other techniques do make that distinction. The approach is also potentially misleading as the trend line ignores the seasonal (i.e. monthly in this example) variations.

Quick test

1. How do you think this approach could be applied to figures on unemployment or changes in retail prices?

Section 4 — Time series analysis

What are you studying?
So far we have used moving averages to identify an underlying trend. In this section we take the analysis a stage further by breaking the trend into its component parts.

How will you be assessed on this?
You will be expected to use the time series approach to calculate the trend figures (as shown in the previous section) and also calculate cyclical, seasonal and residual variations. This section explains how to do this.

There are two types of times series model, the additive model and the multiplicative model. We will focus on the additive model in this text.

> Crucial concept   The **additive model** assumes that the time series can be expressed by the following combination of components:
>
> Value of time series = Trend component + Seasonal component + Residual component
>
> (A long-term cyclical component may also be included, but most examples do not include sufficient data to determine this.)

Let's take our example from the previous section and carry out further analysis to determine the different components. The centred moving average gave us a trend through the time series. If we compare the centred moving average with the actual value for each week, we can determine the seasonal variation.

> Crucial tip   Don't be led into thinking that a seasonal variation must relate to seasons of the year. It simply relates fluctuation observed for the particular business, and it can be over seven days, a month, six months, etc.

We can add another three columns to the table we had earlier:

Week		Cheques	Centred monthly MA	Seasonal variation	Seasonal average	Residual fluctuation
Jan	1	50				
	2	20				
	3	25	43.75	−18.75	−18.10	−0.65
	4	80	44.38	35.63	36.70	−1.08
Feb	1	50	45.63	4.38	3.20	−1.18
	2	25	46.88	−21.88	−21.80	−0.07
	3	30	47.50	−17.50		
	4	85	47.50	37.50		
Mar	1	50	48.13	1.88		
	2	25				
	3	35				
	4	100				

Seasonal variation

This is found by subtracting the centred moving average from the actual value for that period. For example, for January week 3, the seasonal variation is $25 - 43.75 = -18.75$.

Seasonal average

If this approach is to be used to make a reliable prediction, it is important to take account of as much data as possible. We should therefore work out average variations for each 'season', taking the mean of all the seasonal variations for the periods that we have information on. For example, as the pattern is four-weekly, our 'seasons' are week 1, week 2, week 3 and week 4. We have worked out the seasonal variation for January week 3 as −18.75, but for February week 3 it is −17.5. An average of these two will give a figure of −18.1, and this can be used in future calculations.

> **Crucial tip** As seasonal variations should have a combined effect of zero, you should add them up to check that this is the case. If they do not sum to zero, you should make adjustments or round the figures until that is achieved. This has already been done in the table above.

Residual variation

Any difference still unaccounted for must be due to residual (or random) variation. This can be found by rearranging the original formula:

Actual value = Trend component + Seasonal component + Residual component

Residual component = Actual value − (Trend + Average seasonal component)

As the table above demonstrates, these figures are often negligible, and some examples will not ask for them to be calculated. For example, the residual variation for January week 3 is

$$25 - (43.75 - 18.1) = -0.65$$

Seasonally adjusted data

You might find some figures referred to in the press as 'seasonally adjusted'. The reason for doing this is that figures from different seasons can be compared, without the seasonal variation distorting the comparison. The approach is used in presenting unemployment statistics, where the non-seasonal influences are assumed to be connected with political activity or economic policy.

> Crucial concept **Seasonally adjusted figures** show the effect of non-seasonal variations by removing the seasonal variations:
>
> Seasonally adjusted figures = Original figures − Seasonal variation

Use of time series for forecasting

We have already seen how adding a moving averages line to a chart can help to give an indication of likely forecast results. If there is significant seasonal variation, this will not give a realistic forecast for each season, as the variation has been averaged out. If we want to make a forecast for the next period in our example, we can use the moving averages to project the underlying trend, and then adjust each week for the appropriate average seasonal variation.

The centred moving average increased from 43.75 to 48.13 between January week 3 and March week 1, which is an average increase over the period of 0.73 per week. So we would expect that trend to produce a figure of 48.13 + (0.73 × 4) in week April 1, = 48.86, and continue increasing by 0.73 thereafter.

Forecasts		Centred moving average	Seasonal variation	Forecast
Apr	1	51.05	3.20	54.25
	2	51.78	−21.80	29.98
	3	52.51	−18.10	34.41
	4	53.24	36.70	89.94

These forecasts look realistic as they continue the trend of a slight increase, but they also reflect the four-weekly cycle with a peak in week 4 and a trough in week 2.

Quick test

If the number of passengers using the trains is highest on Friday afternoons, what kind of variation is this an example of?

Section 5	**Exponential smoothing**

What are you studying?

This is a technique that emphasises the relative importance of recent observations in producing a forecast. In most situations, last month's results are more relevant than observations made nine months ago or two years ago, but the techniques discussed above tend not to make this distinction.

How will you be assessed on this?

This aspect of forecasting is not included in all syllabi and is not as central as the techniques discussed previously in this chapter. However, if this is part of your syllabus, it is potentially a full examination question, and you will need to be able to apply the technique to basic data to derive a forecast figure.

> Crucial concept **Exponential smoothing** is a technique that uses the following formula to produce weighted moving averages:
>
> New forecast = Old forecast + α (Latest observation – Old forecast) where α is the smoothing constant.

The smoothing constant is a matter of choice, but must be a figure between 0 and 1. If a value close to 1 is used, the forecast will be very sensitive to recent conditions.

Example

A company had forecast sales for the previous week of 500 units, but the actual sales were 480 units. If a smoothing constant of 0.3 is used, the forecast for this week will be:

Last week's forecast + 0.3 (Last week's actual – Last week's forecast)

= 500 + 0.3 (448 – 500)

= 500 – 6 = 494 units

The result is that the forecast takes account of the extent to which the previous week's forecast was in error. In this example, as actual sales were less than forecast, we will expect the forecast for this week to reflect that. But as we are using a smoothing constant of 0.3, the forecast is reduced by 6, rather than the full error of 20 units.

> Crucial tip   Check your answer for logic, as it is easy to get + and – signs confused.

Quick test

1. What values can the exponential smoothing constant take?

Answer to Quick test for Section 2

VC	= £675 / 700 units	= 96.4p per unit
FC	= 550 – (200 x 0.964)	= £357.20
Or	= 1,225 – (900 x 0.964)	= £357.40

Crucial examples

1. Using the high-low method, what would be the cost of next month's production if the volume is expected to be 500 kg and production over the past six months has been as follows?

	kg	£
April	480	14,900
May	490	15,300
June	470	14,800
July	510	16,000
August	540	16,600
September	490	15,500

2. What is the moving average for October in the following series, assuming that there is a three-month cycle?

Month	Telephone calls
July	1,000
August	900
September	1,400
October	1,800
November	2,500
December	2,000

3. Assuming that the following data has a four-quarter seasonal variation, what is the seasonal variation for Quarter 3?

	Quarter 1	Quarter 2	Quarter 3	Quarter 4
2000	24	27	30	21
2001	27	30	31	24

4. A shop uses exponential smoothing to forecast the number of items returned by customers. They use a smoothing constant of 0.3. If the forecast number of returns for yesterday was 25 and the actual number was 28, what will be the forecast number of returns for today?

5. Define each of the following terms covered in this chapter:

Additive model   Projection

Exponential smoothing   Qualitative techniques

Forecasting   Quantitative techniques

High-low method   Time series

Moving averages   Seasonally adjusted figures

Prediction

Answers

1.
	kg	£
Low	470	14,800
High	540	16,600

VC = (16,600 − 14,800) / (540 − 470) = £25.71 per kg

FC = 16,600 − (540 × 25.71) = 16,600 − 13,883 = £2,717

Forecast for 500 kg is 2,717 + (500 × 25.71) = £15,572

2. Moving average for October = (1,400 + 1,800 + 2,500) / 3 = 1,900 calls. There is no need to adjust this as there are an odd number of months in the cycle, so the average is already centred on October.

3.

Quarter		Qtr moving ave.	Centred moving ave.	Seasonal var.
1	24			
2	27			
3	30	25.50	25.875	4.125
4	21	26.25	26.625	-5.625
1	27	27.00	27.125	0.125
2	30	27.25	27.625	2.375
3	31	28.00		
4	24			

Seasonal variation for Quarter 3 is +4.125. As there are only eight quarters given, only four seasonal variations can be calculated (i.e. one for each quarter). If more are given, you should take an average for each quarter.

4. Forecast = Yesterday's forecast + α (Yesterday's actual − Yesterday's forecast)

= 25 + 0.3 (28 − 25) = 25 + 0.9 = 25.9 returns (round to 26).

5. Check each of your answers against the Crucial concepts in this chapter

Crucial reading and research

Reading

Curwin, J. and Slater, R. (2002) *Quantitative Methods for Business Decision*, 5th edn. Thomson Learning. See Chapter 14: Time Series (pp. 335–60).

Lucey, T. ('996) *Quantitative Techniques*, 5th edn. Letts Educational. See Chapter 9: Forecasting Time Series Analysis (pp. 146–53).

Research

It is always useful to try and relate the things you learn in a Quantitative Methods course with what is happening around you. There are many cases of data being collected in order to identify patterns and help make forecasts. You should look actively for such examples in the spheres of economics, current affairs, commercial planning, etc. You can consider what patterns are being identified, what techniques are being used to make forecasts, what assumptions are being made, what limitations there are in the analysis, and so on. Some you will find are very sophisticated models (e.g. analysis of economic growth for the country) while others are very simplistic (e.g. predictions of what the top premiership footballers will be earning in a year's time).

STOCK CONTROL

Chapter summary

Stock (or inventory) is one of the major costs in manufacturing and other industries, and therefore needs to be tightly controlled. There are various management techniques involved in controlling stock, such as just-in-time, but in this chapter you will be introduced to statistical methods for assisting managers in making decisions regarding when to purchase stock, how much to purchase, what level of stock to hold, etc.

Studying this chapter will help you to:

- formulate a basic economic order quantity (EOQ) model;

- determine the EOQ in situations of gradual replenishment and stockouts;

- handle price discounts;

- deal with uncertainty in aspects of stock control;

- use EOQ information to calculate costs related to stock.

Assessment targets

Target 1
Determining the EOQ using a graph or formula is a basic requirement for dealing with EOQ problems in assessments. There are often marks for identifying the EOQ, and then further marks for additional aspects, but these additional calculations are usually dependent on first solving the EOQ problem. This topic is tested in Question 2 at the end of this chapter.

Target 2
Determining the EOQ with gradual replenishment or buffer stocks are two of the additional aspects that might be asked for and which build on the basic EOQ calculation. Question 3 at the end of this chapter tests you on this area.

Target 3
Determining the EOQ where discounts are available is a further refinement to the simple model which reflects real-life situations and which can be used as part of an assessment. You will find Question 4 at the end of this chapter is an example of this type.

Crucial concepts

These are the key terms and concepts you will meet in this chapter:

Buffer stock	Ordering costs
Economic order quantity (EOQ)	Reorder levels
Holding costs	Stockouts
Lead time	

Relevant links

This is a relatively self-contained topic, but the main formula involved is based on differential calculus. It is not necessary to understand this derivation in order to solve stock control problems, but some students might find it useful to link the two topics to deepen their understanding of stock control. For the majority of students this is not necessary.

Section 1   The basic EOQ model

What are you studying?
In this section we will look at the assumptions behind the EOQ model and how to determine the EOQ by using a graph or simple formula.

How will you be assessed on this?
Most examinations provide the EOQ formula, so it is not essential to learn it by heart. You will be expected to be able to identify the relevant figures in the question to apply in the formula, and in some cases it will be necessary first of all to do some calculations to determine the figures. You

may also need to comment on the results by explaining any limitations, assumptions, etc.; so it is important to appreciate the context of the formula as well as being able to apply it.

> Crucial concept The **economic order quantity (EOQ)** is the ordering quantity that minimises the balance of cost between holding costs and ordering costs.

The main assumptions behind the basic EOQ formula are listed below, but some of them will be revised as we look at variations on the model later in this chapter:

- The purchase price remains constant.
- Demand remains constant.
- Replenishment is made instantaneously.
- The cost for each order placed is fixed.
- Holding costs are proportional to average stocks.
- No stockouts are allowed.

> Crucial concepts A **stockout** occurs where stock is allowed to reduce to zero and the company cannot therefore meet demand immediately.
> The **holding cost** is simply the cost associated with having stock over a period of time, and in practice can be made up of interest on capital, storage space, storage equipment, administration costs, etc.
> Similarly, **ordering costs** are incurred each time an order is placed, and can include some administration costs, costs of receiving goods, set up of machinery, etc.

The main reason that working out the EOQ is necessary is that ordering costs and holding costs work in opposite directions. If a company orders a **large** amount each time, it reduces the number of orders each year and therefore reduces the cost of ordering. However, if it orders a **small** amount each time, it reduces the average amount of stock being held during the year and therefore keeps down the cost of holding stock. A mathematical approach is required to see what is the ideal order quantity that balances these two competing pressures. This can be seen in Figure 8.1.

Figure 8.1 could be used to estimate what the EOQ is, as the bottom of the total cost curve must indicate minimum cost. In this example the EOQ would appear to be about 10,000 units. However, a more accurate assessment of the EOQ can be achieved using a formula.

The basic EOQ model centres on a formula that determines the size of order that should be placed, assuming that the organisation wishes to keep costs to a minimum. The formula is

$$\sqrt{\frac{2CD}{H}}$$

where C = ordering cost per order;
        D = demand per annum;
        H = cost of holding one unit in stock for one year.

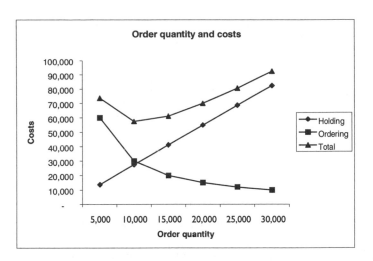

Figure 8.1 Order quantity and costs

Example

A company has calculated that demand for an item is 25,000 units per annum. They know that the cost of placing an order for the item is £65, and that holding costs are 21% of the unit price per unit of average stock per annum. If the unit price is £4.50, what is the EOQ for this item?

$$EOQ = \sqrt{\frac{2CD}{H}} = \sqrt{\frac{2 \times 65 \times 25000}{0.21 \times 4.5}} = 1,855 \text{ units}$$

In other words, the company should place an order for 1,855 units each time it requires this item, which means it will need to place on average 13.5 orders each year.

Quick test

1. Write down two examples of ordering costs and holding costs.

Section 2	Gradual replenishment and buffer stocks

What are you studying?
In this section we take things a stage further by modifying the assumptions given for the basic EOQ model.

How will you be assessed on this?
An examination standard question is unlikely to limit itself to the basic EOQ model, and the introduction of gradual replenishment and/or buffer stocks into a problem are typical ways of increasing the level of difficulty in the question.

It is sometimes helpful to consider these issues visually. A simple line chart, analysing the level of stock over time, gives an easily understood picture of what is happening in a stock control situation. Using the assumptions of the basic EOQ model, the chart would look like Figure 8.2.

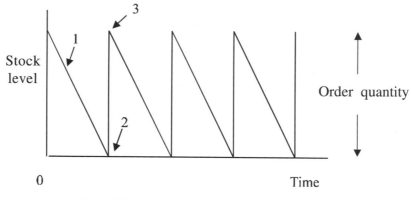

Figure 8.2 Analysis of stock levels over time

This pattern illustrates the gradual depletion of stock, in a constant linear manner (1), the reduction of the stock level to zero before any replacement stock is acquired (2), and the instant replenishment of the stock from zero to the full amount of the order placed (3).

This raises several questions when you try and relate this representation with what is likely to happen in reality. The first issue is whether it is realistic to reach the zero stock level and then instantly receive an order in full, then place no more orders until zero stock is reached again. It may be more realistic to expect stock to be received over a period of time, particularly if the company produces this internally. Secondly, can a company actually allow stocks to reach zero? If there are risks associated with this policy (both financial and operational), then the company may choose to always have some stock 'just in case'. The chart can be modified to take account of these different approaches as in Figure 8.3.

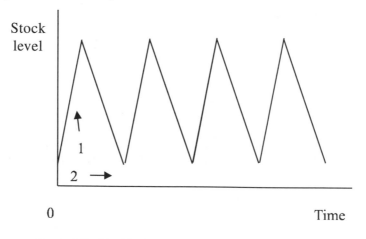

Figure 8.3 Modified analysis of stock levels over time

Instead of a vertical line indicating the instant receipt of stock, the sloping lines (1) show the net rate of replenishment. It is a **net** rate as the stock is being replenished and being used at the same time. Also in this diagram, the stock level is not being allowed to reach zero (2). The minimum level being maintained is known as the **buffer stock** (or safety stock).

To deal with the gradual replenishment illustrated in Figure 8.3, the basic EOQ formula needs to be modified slightly. In the basic model, the cost of holding stock is related to the average stock holding over the year. In this revised model, some units will be taken out of stock for use, even while stock is being replenished. This usage affects the average stock holding and needs to be factored in to the formula, so that:

$$EOQ = \sqrt{\frac{2CD}{H(1-D/R)}}$$

where R is the amount of stock that would be produced in one year's continuous production.

For example, a company has the capability of producing a component in its own factory, and can produce 100,000 per annum. Setting up the machinery etc. to produce a batch of components costs £100 per batch. The costs of holding the components is 10% of the value of the components. The current value of one component is £25. The company requires 75,000 components per annum.

> **Crucial tip** This formula is a bit more unwieldy now, and you might find it helpful to calculate the section $(1 - D/R)$ separately and then insert the solution in the appropriate part of the overall formula.

$$1 - D/R = 1 - 75,000/100,000 = 1 - 0.75 = 0.25$$

$$EOQ = \sqrt{\frac{2CD}{H(1-D/R)}} = \sqrt{\frac{2 \times 100 \times 75000}{2.5 \times 0.25}} = \sqrt{\frac{15,000,000}{0.625}}$$

$$= 4,899 \text{ components}$$

Having a buffer stock is partly to do with maintaining constant production and keeping good customer relations, but can also be looked at as a cost minimisation question. We have already seen that holding stock incurs some costs. But running out of stock can also result in costs, such as lost customer orders or paying a premium for rushing through emergency orders.

> **Crucial concept** The **lead time** is the time taken from placing an order till the stock is received. In the basic EOQ model it is assumed to be zero (i.e. instant receipt of goods).

The issue of buffer stocks is at least partly to do with uncertainty. If all aspects of stock control were known with certainty, then there would never be a need for a buffer stock. However, uncertainty can occur in aspects such as lead times, and also through variability of demand for items. In order to incorporate this uncertainty into stock control problems, it is necessary to attach probabilities to different possible outcomes. The following example illustrates this point.

Example

A trading company has analysed the lead times for one of its products and has found that there is some variation. It wants to know what is the most cost effective reorder level for the item, taking this variation into account. Demand is known to be 10 units per day, and stockout costs are calculated at £12 per unit of unfilled demand. Holding costs are £40 per annum and on average the company places five orders per annum. The lead times are:

Lead time (days)	Probability
2	0.25
3	0.4
4	0.2
5	0.15

In order to solve this problem, we need to identify what the extra costs will be if the company holds a higher level of stock than the minimum (i.e. has a buffer stock) and compare that with the costs saved by avoiding stockouts. The minimum demand during the lead time will be 20 units, because the minimum lead time is two days and demand is 10 units per day. This must also be the minimum reorder level – i.e. the company must reorder when stock reaches 20 units, otherwise a stockout is certain. The company has the option of ordering earlier, so we need to analyse the costs that will result from higher reorder levels, taking the associated probabilities into account.

> Crucial concept   The **reorder level** is the level of stock that indicates an order needs to be placed so that the replacement stock arrives before stock reaches either zero or the buffer stock level.

The possible levels of demand, and therefore reorder levels, using the information on lead times, are as follows:

Lead time (days)	Demand (units)	Probability
2	20	0.25
3	30	0.4
4	40	0.2
5	50	0.15

The costs of stockouts associated with each reorder level are:

Reorder level (units)	Costs	
20	$(10 \times 0.4 + 20 \times 0.2 + 30 \times 0.15) \times £12 \times 5$ orders	= £750
30	$(10 \times 0.2 + 20 \times 0.15) \times £12 \times 5$	= £300
40	$(10 \times 0.15) \times £12 \times 5$	= £90
50		= Nil

The costs are calculated by asking the question, if we reorder at this level, what are the chances of requiring more than this amount in the period between placing the order and receiving the stock? For example, if we reorder at 20 units, there is a 0.4 probability that we will actually need 30, therefore we will be 10 units short. There is also a 0.2 probability that we will be 20 units short, and 0.15 probability that the shortfall will be 30 units short. Each unit we are short costs the company £12, and this could happen each time an order is placed (i.e. five times per annum). The higher the reorder level, the less likelihood there is of a stockout and therefore the less the stockout costs in the table.

The other relevant cost is for holding stock, and this time costs will be higher for higher reorder levels. The minimum reorder level is 20, but above that the company will incur an additional £40 for each additional unit of stock, which means £400 if the reorder level is 30 units, and so on. Putting stockout and holding costs together, we can identify the ideal reorder level for the company:

Reorder level (units)	Stockout costs £	Holding costs £	Total relevant costs £
20	750	Nil	750
30	300	400	700
40	90	800	890
50	Nil	1,200	1,200

Therefore the most cost-effective reorder level for the company, according to this information, is 30 units.

Quick test

1. What is the EOQ if ordering costs are £200 per order, holding costs are £9 per item per year, and demand is 14,500 units?

(Answer at the end of the chapter.)

Section 3   Discounts for large orders

What are you studying?
In previous examples, one of the assumptions made was that the price per unit of stock is constant irrespective of the quantity ordered each time. It is more realistic to allow for reduced prices (discounts) for bulk orders. In this section, we look at how to calculate the EOQ where discounts are available.

How will you be assessed on this?
As this is a realistic scenario, and as it allows examiners to develop an EOQ problem beyond the basic model, it is a favourite approach for designing a demanding assessment. As well as testing your ability to apply a formula, you are also required to identify what figures in the question are relevant and how they should be used. So it is a test of your ability to analyse information logically rather than simply follow a process by rote.

The first step is normally to calculate the EOQ in the usual way, using whatever price is given in the problem as the normal price. This gives you a reference to use in comparison with discounts. If the EOQ is below the discount level, you will then need to identify the costs associated with the EOQ at the normal price with the costs at the discount level (or levels if there is a variety of possible discounts). It is then basically a costing process rather than statistical.

> **Crucial tip** It is essential to only consider the marginal costs in the EOQ calculation, i.e. only those that change as a result of ordering or holding more or less stock. Fixed costs, e.g. the salary of the stores manager, should not be included in your calculations, even if they are given in a question.

Example

A government agency uses 10,000 reams of paper each year, which it purchases on an ad hoc basis for £3 per ream. The manager wishes to cut down on administration costs and is looking into the possibility of making savings in the use of paper. It has been worked out that it costs £20 to place an order (telephone calls, completing forms, etc.) and holding costs are 25% of the purchase price. A discount of 5% is available from a supplier if orders are 1,000 reams or more.

$$\text{EOQ based on normal price} = \sqrt{\frac{2CD}{H}} = \sqrt{\frac{2 \times 20 \times 10,000}{3 \times 0.25}} = 731 \text{ reams}$$

This is less than the discount level of 1,000 reams, so we need to calculate the costs at both levels to identify which is cheaper. This can be done in tabular format.

Order quantity	731 reams	£	1,000 reams	£
Price per unit	£3		£2.85	
Number of orders	10,000/731 = 13.7		10,000/1,000 = 10	
Ordering costs	13.7 × £20	274	10 × £20	200
Average stock	731/2 = 365.5 reams		1,000/2 = 500 reams	
Holding costs	365.5 × £3 × 25%	274	500 × £2.85 × 25%	356
Purchase costs	10,000 × £3	30,000	10,000 × £2.85	28,500
Total costs		30,548		29,056

So in this example there is a saving to be made from ordering in larger amounts and obtaining the bulk order discount as the reduction in purchase costs is greater than the net increase in ordering/holding costs.

> **Crucial tip** Holding costs are often related to average stocks. To work out average stock, simply take the order quantity and divide by two.

Quick test

1. Explain why it might not always be in the best interest of a company to order stock in bulk so that they can obtain a discount on the order.

2. Why would the cost renting a warehouse for storing stock not be a relevant cost in calculating EOQ?

Answer to Quick test for Section 2
EOQ is 803 units.

Crucial examples

1. (a) Give four assumptions that are made in the application of the basic EOQ model.

    (b) What is the purpose of a buffer stock?

2. A wholesale company dealing in footballs has established that demand is 20,000 footballs per month, the cost of storage is £0.80 per annum, and administration costs for placing orders are £25 per order. What is the economic order quantity?

3. A company deals in buying and selling upmarket camcorders. The holding cost for one unit is £22 per annum, and the cost of not being able to satisfy a sales order from stock is £50 (i.e. per unit per unfilled order). The lead time for the camcorders is two days, and demand in the lead time is as follows:

Demand	Probability
0	0.55
1	0.3
2	0.1
3	0.05

    The company orders stock every two months. What is the reorder level that would minimise total costs?

4. (a) Company Alpha has the following information for its stock. Using this information, what is the EOQ?

Ordering cost	£50 per order
Price	£5 per unit
Holding cost	25% of unit price

    (b) If the following discounts are available to Company Alpha, what order quantity would result in the lowest total cost?

Orders up to 2,999 units	No discount
3,000 to 5,999 units	5% discount
6,000 units and above	6% discount

5. Explain each of these terms:

Buffer stock	Reorder levels
Economic order quantity (EOQ)	Ordering costs
Holding costs	Stockouts
Lead time	

Answers

1. (a) The purchase price remains constant; demand remains constant; replenishment is made instantaneously; the cost for each order placed is fixed; holding costs are proportional to average stocks; no stockouts are allowed.

    (b) A buffer stock helps a company to avoid stockouts in situations with variable demand

and/or variable lead times. In normal circumstances the buffer stock will not be needed, but it is available for emergencies or extraordinary circumstances.

2. $\sqrt{\dfrac{2CD}{H}} = \sqrt{\dfrac{2 \times 25 \times 240{,}000}{0.8}} = 3{,}873$

3. The costs of stockouts associated with each reorder level are:

Reorder level	Costs	
0	$(1 \times 0.3 + 2 \times 0.1 + 3 \times 0.05) \times £50 \times 6$ orders	= £195
1	$(1 \times 0.1 + 2 \times 0.05) \times £50 \times 6$	= £60
2	$(1 \times 0.05) \times £50 \times 6$	= £15
3		= Nil

Additional holding costs are £22 per unit, giving total costs of:

Reorder level (units)	Stockout costs £	Holding costs £	Total relevant costs costs £
0	195	Nil	195
1	60	22	82
2	15	44	59
3	Nil	66	66

A reorder level of one unit is therefore recommended.

4. (a) $EOQ = \sqrt{\dfrac{2 \times 50 \times 18{,}000}{0.25 \times 5}} = 1{,}200$

(b)

Order quantity	1,200	£	3,000	£	6,000	£
Purchase price	£5		£4.75		£4.70	
Number of orders	15		6		3	
Ordering costs		750		300		150
Average stock (units)	600		1,500		3,000	
Holding costs	600 × £5 × 0.25	750	1,500 × £4.75 × 0.25	1,781	3,000 × £4.70 × 0.25	3,525
Purchase costs	18,000 × £5	90,000	18,000 × £4.75	85,500	18,000 × £4.70	84,600
Total costs		91,500		87,581		88,275

Therefore 3,000 units is the most cost effective order quantity, given the available discounts.

5. Check your answers against the **Crucial concepts** in this chapter.

Crucial reading and research

Reading

These books provide further information and examples on stock control and related issues:

Curwin, J. and Slater, R. (2002) *Quantitative Methods for Business Decisions*, 5th edn. Thomson Learning. See Chapter 21: Modeling Stock Control and Queues (pp. 514–23).

Drury, C. (2000) *Management and Cost Accounting*, 5th edn. Chapman & Hall. See Chapter 26. Quantitative Models for Planning and Control of Stocks (pp. 994–1004).

Lucey, T. (1996) *Quantitative Techniques*, 5th edn. Letts Educational. See Chapters 11 to 14, in particular Chapter 13: Inventory Control – Economic Order Quantity and Chapter 14: Safety Stock and Reorder Levels (pp. 204–23).

Research

You might find it useful to look into related topics, particularly different management issues related to stock control. There are a number of different techniques associated with stock, including the two-bin system, periodic review, 'just-in-time' (JIT), total quality management (TQM), etc. Some syllabi expect students to be able to discuss these approaches as well as being competent in the numerical aspects of stock control, but in this chapter we have focused on the latter.

LINEAR PROGRAMMING

Chapter summary

Allocation problems are concerned with situations where resources are scarce and need to be utilised to their best advantage. Linear programming (LP) is one of the allocation techniques, and it involves a procedure to optimise some objective where some of the resources are subject to some constraint.

Studying this chapter will help you to:

- formulate LP problems in a standardised manner;
- solve LP problems using the graphical method or equations;
- deal with both maximising and minimising problems.

Assessment targets

Target 1

In your assessment you may be asked to identify the optimal allocation of resources by using the graphical method. To do this you need to formulate the problem correctly, show the information in a graph and interpret the graph to find the solution. Question 1 (a) and 1 (b) at the end of this chapter test your ability to solve LP problems using this graphical method.

Target 2

The same answer obtained using the graphical method can be obtained by solving the linear equations. An examination question may specify that this approach is required. Question 1 (c) at the end of this chapter tests your ability to solve LP problems using equations.

Target 3

Once you have solved a LP problem, you might need to work out if it would be worth paying extra to obtain more of the resources that are the main constraints in your solution. Question 1 (d) at the end of this chapter tests that you can identify the value of scarce resources.

Crucial tip	When you are studying, it can be useful to solve problems using both methods to check that you have the right answer. In an examination you would not normally have time to do both.

Crucial concepts

These are the key terms and concepts you will meet in this chapter:

Constraints	Optimal solution
Contribution	Shadow price
Feasible region	Simultaneous equations
Objective function	Slack

Relevant links

This is a self-contained topic, and the technique is used in very specific circumstances. The chapter can be studied without detailed knowledge of other chapters in this study guide. Links to other specialised variations on this technique not covered in this study guide are given at the end of the chapter.

Section 1	**Solving LP problems using the graphical method and equations**

What are you studying?

In this section we will look at the fundamental tasks involved in interpreting a linear programming problem, stating it in mathematical terms so that we can use the approach, and determining a solution using graphs and equations.

How will you be assessed on this?

You need to be able to apply all the steps in this approach to answer an exam question where there are two variables (e.g. two possible products) and where the use of the graphical method is either required or implied. More complex problems require the use of the simplex method, and transportation and assignment models are used in specific situations. You need to be able to recognise from the information in a question which method should be used

A common management decision for companies that produce more than one product is how much of each product to make during a period. This decision becomes more critical when one or more of the resources required to make the products is scarce. In simple situations, this decision is made by calculating the **contribution** per unit of scarce resource.

> **Crucial concept** The **contribution** per unit is the difference between the selling price of a product and the variable costs involved in making one unit of the product. It is a very useful figure for assisting in decision-making.

Suppose a company makes two products, A and B, and the standards per unit are as follows:

Product A	£	£	Product B	£	£
Selling price		38	Selling price		42
Materials (8 @ £1)	8		Materials (4 @ £1)	4	
Labour (6 @ £2)	12		Labour (8 @ £2)	16	
Machine costs (4 @ £1)	4	24	Machine costs (6 @ £1)	6	26
Contribution		14	Contribution		16

Labour hours have been limited in the next period to 2,880. No other inputs are constrained, but the company does not expect to sell more than 420 units of Product A. As labour is the scarce resource, we need to look at the contribution per unit of labour for each product.

> **Crucial tip** LP assumes that products are infinitely divisible (i.e. that it is possible to produce 14.98 units of a product). In most cases you will want to adjust your answers to whole numbers to have a solution that makes sense.

Product A uses 6 labour hours and makes a contribution of £14, therefore the contribution per labour hour is £2.33. Product B uses 8 labour hours and makes a contribution of £16, therefore contribution per labour hour is £2.00. Since A makes the greater contribution per labour hour then the company should allocate scarce resources to A first.

However, we know that we do not expect to sell more than 420 units of A in the next period, so we can assume that 420 is the maximum we want to produce. To make 420 units requires 2,520 labour hours (420 x 6). The balance of 360 labour hours should be used to make B, and as B needs 8 labour hours then the company should make 45 units (i.e. 360/8). The company can therefore maximise its contribution (and hence its profits) by making 420 units of A and 45 units of B in the next period. This will generate a contribution of: (£14 x 420) + (£16 x 45) = £6,600

> **Crucial concept** In LP problems it is essential to identify clearly the **constraints** (or limitations) that affect the achievement of the stated objective.

The situation becomes more complicated if we add another constraint. Let's assume that the two products A and B use the same material, and that material availability in the next period will be restricted to 3,440 units. And a further constraint exists in the form of machine time, which is limited to 2,760 hours. Using the same method as before we can calculate the contributions per unit of scarce resource, i.e.

	Product A	Product B
Labour	£2.33	£2.00
Materials	£1.75	£4.00
Machine	£3.50	£2.67

If we are to refer only to the labour constraint then we should make A up to the total likely sales. But B contributes more from the materials point of view. It is not immediately clear how we should proceed in this situation, but dealing with multiple constraints is where LP can help.

Step 1

The first step is to define what we are trying to optimise. In this situation we are trying to optimise the contribution made by the products, so our objective is to maximise contribution. Because LP is a mathematical technique, we need to formulate the problem in mathematical terms. This involves expressing the objective and all the constraints as formulae.

> Crucial tip As this is a mathematical model you need to be careful to specify constraints that seem common sense, otherwise the solution might include negative quantities of a product.

> Crucial concept The **objective function** is a mathematical statement of the objective of the LP problem. Each LP problem can only have a single objective.

The objective function expresses the objective in terms of the variables that objective is dependent on. In this case the variables are the amounts of A and B the company is going to produce. So for this problem the objective function will be:

Maximise C (contribution) = $14A + 16B$, subject to the following constraints:

$$8A + 4B \leq 3,440 \qquad \text{(material constraint)}$$
$$6A + 8B \leq 2,880 \qquad \text{(labour constraint)}$$
$$4A + 6B \leq 2,760 \qquad \text{(machine capacity)}$$
$$0 \leq A \leq 420 \qquad \text{(minimum and maximum sales of A)}$$
$$Z \geq 0 \qquad \text{(minimum sales)}$$

Step 2

Next, we need to draw the axes of the graph that represent the two unknowns, in this case A and B, and draw each constraint as a separate line on the graph. To do this, you should replace A and B with zero separately in each equation to identify where the line meets each axis. For example, using the material constraint equation (note that we can use = here rather than ≤ as we are drawing the line that represents the boundary of this constraint), everything below and to the left of this line will represent the area that does not breach this constraint:

8A + 4B = 3,440
If A = 0, then B = 3,440/4 = 860
If B = 0, then A = 3,440/8 = 430

> **Crucial tip** You can do anything to an equation without disturbing it provided that you do it to both sides.

This line can now be drawn on the graph to show the area representing combinations of producing A and B. Adding the other constraint lines onto the same graph shows the area of possible production, known as the **feasible region**, as indicated by the shaded area in the graph in Figure 9.1. The constraints preventing negative production are automatically included as the graph only shows positive values.

> **Crucial concept** The **feasible region** is the area on the graph that does not contravene any of the constraints and is therefore the area containing all possible production plans.

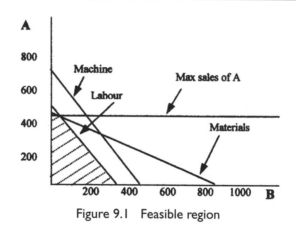

Figure 9.1   Feasible region

Step 3

Now that we have identified the feasible region, it is necessary to find the point in or on the edge of the feasible region that maximises the objective function. This can be done by plotting the objective function line using any reasonable values of A and B within the feasible region to get started, and then plotting parallel lines at successively greater values until the line leaves the feasible region. The last vertex (point where two constraint lines meet) to be touched represents the optimal solution.

> **Crucial concept** The **optimal solution** is the solution that gives the highest value for what we are trying to maximise (e.g. contribution) without breaching any of the constraints in the problem.

The graph in Figure 9.1 makes it clear that some of the constraints might be redundant, i.e. they do not affect the feasible region as there are other more severe constraints. The two lines for maximum sales of A and machine capacity to not touch the feasible region, and so in this example they are redundant. The optimal solution must therefore lie at one of the following vertices shown in Figure 9.2.

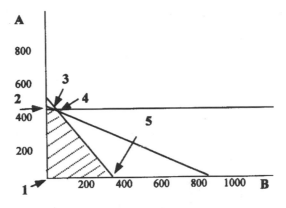

Figure 9.2   Possible locations of optimal solution

- Vertex 1 – This would mean producing zero units of both A and B and is not likely to be the optimal solution.
- Vertex 2 – This is the intersection of the maximum sales of A line and the A axis and would involve producing 420 units of A and none of B.
- Vertex 3 – This is the intersection of the maximum sales of A line and the materials constraint line. Again production of A would be 420, and from the graph production of B would appear to be about 20.
- Vertex 4 – This is the intersection of the constraint lines for labour and materials. Production would be approximately 400 of A and 60 of B.
- Vertex 5 – This is the intersection of the labour constraint line and the B axis. Production would be none of A and 360 of B.

Crucial tip	It is easier to draw the objective function if you choose a value that is divisible by the coefficients in the equation. So, in this example, if we choose a value divisible by 14 and 16 we can easily plot the points where the line intersects the two axes. Remember, this line is just a starting point, so you can have several attempts at producing something reasonable.

Using the coefficients of the objective function, 14 and 16, gives a value of 224. This is not likely to give us a line far enough to the right in the graph (bearing in mind that we expect to have a solution giving production of 300 or more of one of the products) so we can multiply this by 10 or even 20 to give a more realistic line.

Plotting this line, as for the constraints, can be achieved by finding the intercepts of the line with the two axes:

$$14A + 16B = 4,480$$
$$\text{If } A = 0, B = 4,480/16 = 280$$
$$\text{If } B = 0, A = 4,480/14 = 320$$

This is shown as the dotted line in Figure 9.3.

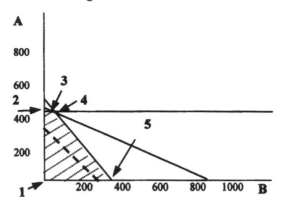

Figure 9.3   Plotting the objective function

What we need to do effectively is keep plotting lines that still satisfy this equation but with higher values until we leave the feasible region. As these lines must all be parallel, this can be done by eye. Place a ruler along the line that has already been drawn and move it upwards and to the right (because we are trying to **maximise** the objective, so we want the highest possible values of A and B), keeping it parallel at all times to the original line. Note the vertices it crosses as you move it until you reach the last vertex. If the graph has been drawn accurately, this represents the optimal solution as it is the point at the edge of the feasible region that gives the highest value for the objective function. This means it must give us the greatest contribution in this example.

As the ruler is moved right and up, it crosses vertex 5, then 2, then 3 and finally vertex 4. Vertex 1, as pointed out above, was never likely to be the answer. We now need to work out the actual values of A and B at this point. This can be done approximately by reading off the graph, and above it was suggested this would give 400 A and 60 B. As this is the overall solution to the problem, we would want a more specific answer, and this can be obtained by simultaneous equations.

> Crucial concept Solving **simultaneous equations** involves using two equations (or more) that have the same unknown variables. The basic method is to eliminate one of the two unknowns between the equations. This is achieved by restating one of the equations so that one of the unknowns has the same coefficient in both equations and then adding or subtracting the equations to eliminate it.

The two equations at vertex 4 are the constraints for labour and materials:

$$8A + 4B = 3,440 \quad \text{(materials)}$$
$$6A + 8B = 2,880 \quad \text{(labour)}$$

If we multiply the materials equation by 2 we can then easily eliminate B by subtracting one equation from the other:

$$16A + 8B = 6,880 \quad \text{(materials)}$$
$$6A + 8B = 2,880 \quad \text{(labour)}$$

Subtracting labour from materials gives:

10A = 4,000, so A = 400

Then substituting in either equation to solve for B, e.g. using the labour equation:

(6 x 400) + 8B	= 2,880
2,400 + 8B	= 2,880
8B	= 480
B	= 60

Thus we should make 400 units of A and 60 units of B if we want to maximise our contribution (and hence our profits). At this level of production we will earn:

(400 x 14) + (60 x 16) = £6,560

> **Crucial tip**   Using the graphical method is not always easy, particularly if two or more of the vertices at the edge of the feasible region are very close to each other (as with 3 and 4 in this example). If there is any doubt which is the optimal solution when you use the objective function line in the graph, you can use simultaneous equations to solve for two vertices and the one with the higher value is the optimal solution.

Quick test

1. A company makes two products. X costs £50 to make and sells for £80, while Y sells for 40% above its cost of £30. How would you express the objective function assuming the company wishes to maximise profit?

2. In a maximisation problem, having drawn all the constraints on a graph, how would you identify the optimal point?

Section 2   Valuation of scarce resources

What are you studying?
In some situations one or more of the constraints are redundant and therefore do not affect the feasible region. And usually only two resources meet at the optimal solution, and so for all other resources there is some slack. In this section we look at the question whether it is worth paying extra to obtain more of the scarce resources and increase our objective.

How will you be assessed on this?
Being able to derive the optimal solution as described in Section 1 above is all that is required in some examinations, but it is possible for you to be asked to do this as the first part of the question, and then separately consider the value of the scarce resources to derive an alternative solution.

Crucial concept **Slack** is the amount by which a particular resource is under-utilised. It occurs where the optimal solution is not effectively constrained by the availability of this resource, i.e. the optimal solution does not fall on the constraint line for this resource.

In our previous example we were not constrained by machine hours nor by the maximum sales of A line. This suggests that if we could move the material and labour constraints (i.e. obtain more of these resources somehow) then we might be able to increase our contribution. However, it is possible that we may have to pay a premium for these additional resources. So we need to identify what it would be worth paying to obtain the additional amounts.

What we are effectively asking is what will be the optimal solution if we have one additional unit of material? This would make the material constraint:

$$8A + 4B = 3,441$$

This gives us a new line, slightly higher than before, intersecting the B axis at 860.25 and the A axis at 430.125. As the line has moved only very slightly, it will still intersect the labour constraint, and therefore we can solve these two equations simultaneously as before to give:

$$6A + 8B = 2,880 \quad \text{(labour)}$$
$$8A + 4B = 3,441 \quad \text{(material)}$$

$$6A + 8B = 2,880$$
$$16A + 8B = 6,882 \quad \text{(material x 2)}$$

$$10A = 4,002 \text{ so, } A = 400.2$$

$$(8 \times 400.2) + 4B = 3,441$$
$$3,201.6 + 4B = 3,441$$
$$4B = 239.4, \text{ so } B = 59.85$$

So we should now produce 400.2 units of A and 59.85 units of B to maximise contribution. The new solution involves producing more of A and less of B. We can calculate the change in contribution arising out of acquiring 1 extra unit of material (at the same prices as before) as:

Increase in contribution from A (£14 x 0.2)	£2.80
Reduction in contribution from B (£16 x 0.15)	£2.40
Increase in contribution	£0.40

This is known as the **shadow price** of materials. In reality, material has been identified as scarce and to obtain more will normally cost more. So the most we would be willing to pay to acquire more materials is an extra 39p per unit, because paying an extra 40p would cancel out the increased contribution.

Crucial concept The value of an independent marginal increase in a resource is called the **shadow price**.

Only a scarce resource can have a shadow price (there is no point in paying extra for a resource if you already have some of it available), so in this example only labour and materials would be worth paying more for. Eventually, as more of the scarce resource is acquired and the associated line in the graph is moved, it will meet another constraint line (e.g. maximum sales of A) and the resource associated with that line then becomes binding.

Minimising problems

In the above example the objective was to **maximise** the contribution. The graphical method can also be employed where the objective is to minimise something (usually cost). The steps involved in the process are basically the same as those outlined already for the maximisation problem, but there are some differences in the way the graph appears and how it is interpreted.

First, the constraint equations will be in the form $\geq$, and this means that the feasible region will be above and to the right of most of the constraints (whereas in the example above it was below and to the left). Secondly, as the objective is to minimise, the optimal solution will lie at the point furthest to the bottom left that still touches the feasible region. And thirdly, once the objective function line has been drawn, you need to move it left and downwards to identify the optimal solution.

Quick test

1. How would you define slack?
2. Solve the following using simultaneous equations:
   $$10P + 25M = 150$$
   $$16P + 20M = 160$$

Crucial examples

1. (a) Show the following constraint lines plotted on a graph:
      (i) $x \geq 0$
      (ii) $y \geq 150$
      (iii) $x + y \leq 450$
      (iv) $4x + y \leq 600$

   (b) Use the graph to identify the maximum possible value of the following objective function given these constraints: $3x + y$

   (c) Use simultaneous equations to confirm the answer you got in part (b).

   (d) What is the maximum that you would pay for additional units of the resource defined by constraint (iii)?

2. Explain each of the following terms:

Constraints	Optimal solution
Contribution	Shadow price
Feasible region	Simultaneous equations
Objective function	Slack

Answers

1. (a) See Figure 9.4.

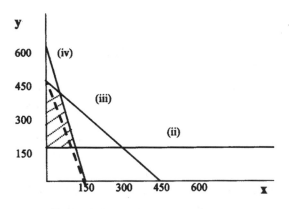

Figure 9.4 Plot of constraint lines

(b) Optimum is at intersection of constraint lines (iii) and (iv), and reading off the graph this would appear to give a solution of approximately 75 x and 375 y. Value of objective function is therefore (3 x 75) + 375 = 600.

(c) Using simultaneous equations, the solution is:

(iv) $4x + y = 600$

(iii) $x + y = 450$

Take (iii) away from (iv):

$3x = 150$

$x = 50$

Substitute in (iii):

$50 + y = 450$

$y = 400$

Value of objective function is (3 x 50) + 400 = 550.

Note that the graphical method gave a reasonable answer, but the accuracy depends on how well the graph has been drawn and how easy it is to read off the values on the two axes.

(d) You need to work out the shadow price of the resource in constraint (iii), so add one unit to the available amount, then solve by simultaneous equations again:

(iv) $4x + y = 600$

(iii) $x + y = 451$

$3x + y = 149$

$x = 49.67$

$49.67 + y = 450$

$y = 400.33$

Value of objective function is now:

(3 x 49.67) + 401.33 = 550.34

You would therefore pay a maximum of 0.33 per unit for extra resources, as paying 0.34 would only maintain the current profit, not increase it.

2. Check your answers against the Crucial concepts in this chapter.

Crucial reading and research

Reading

Curwin, J. and Slater, R. (2002) *Quantitative Methods for Business Decisions*, 5th edn. Thomson Learning. See Chapter 19: Linear Programming (pp. 457–70).

Drury, C. (2000) *Management and Cost Accounting*, 5th edn. Chapman & Hall. See Chapter 26: The Application of Linear Programming to Management Accounting (pp. 1029–37).

Lucey, T. (1996) *Quantitative Techniques*, 5th edn. Letts Educational. See Chapters 16: Linear Programming – Introduction, and Chapter 17: Linear Programming – Graphical Solutions (pp. 243–68).

Research

We have been looking at the basic aspects of linear programming, but it is a technique with some additional and specialised applications. One refinement is dealing with situations where there are more than two variables. As the graphical method is two-dimensional, you would need to use what is called the simplex method to solve such problems. Each of the textbooks mentioned above includes coverage of this aspect of linear programming. Other specialist applications are the transportation and assignment algorithms – and if your syllabus includes these topics, you will find explanations of them in Chapters 20 and 21 of the Lucey text.

As with many quantitative methods, linear programming has been included as a feature of some computer software products. If you have access to software of this kind it can be useful as a way of identifying correct solutions, but remember you need to be able to solve problems without the aid of computers in your examination.

CHAPTER 10

NETWORK
ANALYSIS

Chapter summary

Network analysis is a general term used to cover a variety of techniques. In this chapter we will use the term Critical Path Analysis (CPA), while other texts you might refer to can use terms such as Programme Evaluation and Review Technique (PERT), etc. The common feature of these techniques is that they are used to assist managers in designing, planning and controlling complex projects through representing the elements of the project in diagrams.

Studying this chapter will help you to:

- understand and use the key terms involved in network analysis;
- draw a network using conventional symbols and following generally accepted rules;
- identify the critical path and use this information to draw conclusions about the project;
- use a network to determine earliest start times and latest start times for activities, and also available float and slack;
- use 'normal' and 'crash' information to reduce the projects time and/or costs;
- incorporate probability into network problems.

Assessment targets

Target 1
The ability to draw a network and determine the critical path is a fundamental area of knowledge that is essential for tackling examination questions on network analysis. Question 1 at the end of the chapter requires you to draw a network and determine the duration of the critical path.

Target 2
As well as being able to identify the critical path, you will need to know how to calculate the amount of latitude that exists in the non-critical activities. Your ability to calculate floats and slack is tested in Question 2 at the end of the chapter.

Target 3
Some assessments present information on durations and costs under normal circumstances, plus costs and durations that result from completing activities in less time than normal. Your ability to carry out this process is assessed in Question 3 at the end of the chapter.

Target 4
The final element introduced in this chapter is the use of a range of possible durations for each activity. You need to be able to use this information to draw a network, identify the critical path and calculate the probability of different outcomes. Question 4 at the end of the chapter tests your ability to incorporate uncertainty in determining project duration.

Crucial concepts

These are the key terms and concepts you will meet in this chapter:

Activity	(Total) float
Dummy activity	Slack
Event	Free float
Critical path	Independent float
Crash cost/crash time	Cost slope
	PERT

Relevant links

The main techniques in this chapter relate solely to the topic of network analysis and do not require specific previous knowledge. In **Section 5** we will introduce the idea of uncertainty into the analysis of networks, and this relates to some of the basic aspects of probability discussed in **Chapter 2**.

Section 1	Drawing a simple network

What are you studying?
In this section we will look at the basic elements involved in drawing a network.

How will you be assessed on this?

The information and skills introduced in this section are fundamental to understanding what critical path analysis involves and to drawing the diagrams that are essential for solving CPA problems. Examinations will normally take things a stage further than producing a simple network, and these variations are discussed in later sections.

It is important that you are able to use the appropriate symbols and follow certain conventions in the way that you draw networks. As well as being necessary for correctly solving a network problem, there are also usually some marks available in an exam for the correct presentation of the information.

> Crucial concept A **network** is a combination of activities and events, graphically depicted in a logical sequence according to set rules.

A network is essentially a collection of activities, presented in a way that shows how the activities are interrelated, thus providing information that can help in planning the overall project. The elements that make up a network are activities and events. The usual convention is to show activities as arrows in the network and show events as circles or 'nodes' (**Note:** There is an alternative approach that shows activities as the nodes, which are connected by arrows. These are referred to as 'activity on node' networks, but the approach is not covered in this text.) For ease of reference, and to prevent networks becoming congested, labels are used to refer to the various activities and events, usually with activities referred to as activity A, activity B, etc., and events being numbered from 0 onwards.

> Crucial concepts An **activity** is an element of the project that needs to be completed in order for the overall project to succeed.
>
> An **event** is a point in time that indicates the beginning and/or ending of activities in the network.

As already mentioned, network diagrams are drawn using various conventions. These ensure that the diagram is logical and complete, and also allow people familiar with the conventions to understand or analyse networks drawn by others. The following are the main conventions:

- Networks are drawn from left to right, and nodes are numbered from left to right.
- Activities are represented by arrows, events by nodes.
- No two nodes may be linked by more than one activity.
- A network must have only one start event and one finish event.
- Every activity must have one preceding and one succeeding event.
- An activity cannot start until its preceding event has been reached.
- An event is not complete until all the activities leading to it are complete.
- All activities must be integrated into the network, i.e. no 'danglers' are allowed where the activity leads to an event that is separate from the remainder of the network indicating that the activity is not actually contributing to the completion of the project.

One of the key steps in drawing a network is to list all the major activities involved in the project showing which activities **must** precede others.

> **Crucial tip**   You cannot draw a network correctly without being absolutely clear on the relationships between activities, in particular knowing for each activity whether it is dependent on one or more other activities. In any problem, take time over this step, otherwise you will be starting with an incorrect network, making all other aspects of the problem more difficult.

Example

The following information relates to making a pie:

Activity	Preceding activity	Description
A		Prepare pastry
B	A	Cook pastry
C	B	Have a glass of wine
D		Prepare topping E
E	B, D	Add topping to pastry
F	E	Decorate

The network diagram is shown in Figure 10.1.

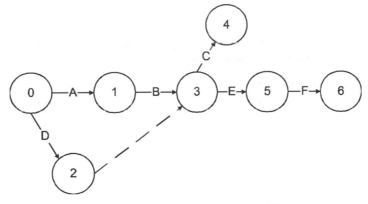

Figure 10.1   Network diagram (1)

Once the network has been drawn, it should be possible to draw some conclusions about how the project should be managed. In this example, we have two activities that can both start at event 0, i.e. at the beginning: i.e. activities A and D. It may not be physically possible to do both activities (we will look at resourcing issues later), but the network shows that it is logically possible. There is also an example of a dangler, i.e. activity C. It may be part of the person's routine to have a glass of wine while baking, and he or she may not allow themselves that luxury until a target has been met (here completing activity B). But it is not an essential part of the process and does not directly contribute to reaching the overall goal, so it should be ignored for planning purposes. We can also see that there are two main 'paths' through the network, i.e. ways of going from the start event on the left to the finish event on the right. These can be described as:

A, B, E, F
D, E, F

In the next section we will look at identifying which of these is 'critical', but in this example we cannot tell as we are not given the times involved in carrying out the various activities. The network also shows an example of a dummy activity, i.e. the activity shown by the dotted arrow connecting events 2 and 3. This activity is required to maintain the logic of the network, showing that activity E is dependent on both activity D and activity B, but it is not a real activity involving time and resources.

> Crucial concept A **dummy activity** is required to represent the logic of the network or to avoid having two activities running between the same two nodes. It is represented by a dotted arrow, and takes no time or resources to complete.

> Crucial tip Networks do not always come out neat and orderly at the first attempt. In an examination you may have to try one or two drafts before getting a network that is correct and easily understood.

Quick test

1. What is a node?
2. Why does a dummy activity not affect the duration of a project?

Section 2   The critical path

What are you studying?
In this section we will look at identifying the critical path through a network and using this to make planning and control decisions.

How will you be assessed on this?
This is a crucial element of CPA, and it is almost certain that any examination question on networks will require use of the critical path. The topics in the later sections of this chapter rely on the critical path for making more sophisticated and complex analyses and decisions.

Activities in networks have durations associated with them. By combining a knowledge of durations with the logical sequence we can calculate the least time it will take to finish the project. There may be more than one critical path in a network.

> Crucial concept The **critical path** is the path through the network that will take the longest to complete.

The importance of the critical path may be summed up as follows:

- It indicates the shortest time in which it is possible to complete the whole project.
- Any delay in any of the activities on this path will also delay the project's completion.
- Allocating further resources to this path may result in reduction in the overall duration of the project (but if that is done, some other path in the network may then become critical).

- It also shows that events not on the critical path are by definition non-critical and there is some latitude in the timing of these activities (see **slack** in Section 3 below).

The first step in the process for calculating the critical path is to calculate the earliest start time (EST) for each activity, i.e. the earliest possible time at which a following activity can start. This is calculated by taking the EST for the **preceding** activity and adding the duration of that activity. Where there is more than one preceding activity, the calculation must be done for each activity and the **latest** of the answers taken as the EST of the next activity. The EST results can be incorporated in the nodes of the network, starting with an EST of 0 for the start event and working from left to right through the network.

The next step is to calculate latest start times (LST), i.e. the latest time at which a preceding activity must be completed without affecting the length of the project. This process works through the network diagram from right to left. The LST for the end event will be the same as the EST. For the other events, it is a case of working backwards through the network, taking the previously calculated LST and subtracting the duration of each activity in turn.

Crucial tip   A check on whether you have done this correctly is to determine the critical path beforehand, and then ensure that the ESTs and LSTs on this path are identical.

For example, a project is made up of the following activities:

Activity	Preceded by	Duration (days)
E		4
F		5
G		7
H	E	3
I	E	2
J	F	2
K	G	10
L	H, I, J	6
M	J	3
N	M, L	6
O	K	3

The resulting network, showing the EST on the left of each node and the LST on the right, looks like Figure 10.2.

Quick test

1. Can there be more than one critical path in a network?

2. Why is knowing the critical path of benefit to a project manager?

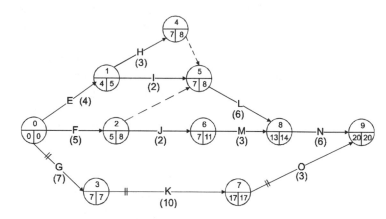

Figure 10.2 Network diagram (2)

Section 3   Float and slack

What are you studying?

Now that you are familiar with drawing a network and identifying the critical path, we can look at the ideas of float and slack. These are sometimes used as though they are the same thing, but in this text we will be making a distinction between the two.

How will you be assessed on this?

Float and slack are related to the topics we have already covered (i.e. critical path, earliest start time, latest start time, etc.), and it is quite common for examination questions to ask you to calculate these in addition to the more basic aspects of drawing and interpreting a network.

> Crucial tip   As definitions of these two terms vary, if you are asked to calculate either float or slack, it is worth defining briefly what you understand by the term(s).

First of all, we will look at float. In the previous section, you saw that the events on the critical path always have identical ESTs and LSTs. When it comes to considering the float, it is the activities that are **not** on the critical path that we will be focusing on. This is because float is to do with the possibility of delaying activities, and we know that activities on the critical path cannot be delayed without affecting the overall length of a project.

> Crucial concept **(Total) float** is the amount of time by which an activity may be delayed (assuming we are disregarding the possible impact on the floats of other activities).

In the previous example, activity I had a float of four days, calculated as follows (see Figure 10.3):

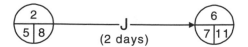

Figure 10.3 Network diagram (3)

LST of following event – EST of preceding event – Duration of activity I

= 11 – 5 – 2 = 4 days

This means that, taking activity I in isolation, because it is not a critical activity we can afford to delay it by four days without affecting the overall duration of the project. If we do the same for activity F, we find that it has a float of three days (see Figure 10.4).

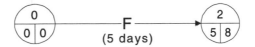

Figure 10.4   Network diagram (4)

However, we could not delay both of these activities by the combined float of seven days. This is because delaying activity F by three days means it will not finish until day 8. This in turn means that activity I cannot start until day 8. We calculated its float by assuming that activity I could start on day 5, but now activity F has eaten into that float, leaving only one of the four days that we originally calculated. This is why the concept of float is sometimes further analysed to take into account the effect of preceding activities and the effect on following activities. In this approach, the figures we calculated for activities I and F would be referred to as **total float**.

Crucial concepts **Free float** is the permissible delay if we do not want to reduce the float available on subsequent activities, but do not mind affecting the floats of preceding activities.

Independent float is the permissible delay if we do not want to affect the floats of any other activities (either preceding or following).

Free float for activity F is calculated as:

EST of following activity – EST of preceding activity – Duration of activity
= 5 – 0 – 5 = nil

Logically, if there is no free float, there cannot be an independent float for the activity, but we can show that is the case using the following approach.

Independent float for activity F would be calculated as:

EST of following activity – LST of preceding activity – Duration of activity
= 5 – 0 – 5 = nil

This explains why delaying activity F by three days reduced the available float for activity I by three days. As there is no free float associated with activity F, we cannot delay it without affecting subsequent activities like activity I.

It is clear, then, that float is being used with reference to activities. Slack, on the other hand, is usually used in relation to events, not activities. All events on the critical path will have zero slack, as there is no difference between the EST and LST of these events.

> Crucial concept **Slack** is the difference between the EST and LST for each event.

Quick test

1. What are the total float, free float and independent float of Activity X?

Activity	EST	LST	Duration	Preceding activity
X	8	9	3	S
Y	17	23	3	X

(Answer at the end of this chapter.)

2. What is the relationship between float and the critical path?

Section 4　Least cost scheduling

What are you studying?

A common feature of managing a complex project is the need to manage cost as well as the duration of the project. So far we have been looking at networks in terms of the time taken for each activity and the overall duration as indicated by the critical path. In this section we will take things a stage further and consider the costs associated with each activity, and therefore the budget required to complete the whole project. This will include distinguishing between the costs that are expected for the 'normal' duration and costs that result from completing activities in less than normal time.

How will you be assessed on this?

As it is common to have a limited budget for carrying out a project, it is often the case that a network analysis scenario will include cost information. This is particularly true if you are studying network analysis as part of a business studies, management or accountancy course. You might be expected to be able to construct the initial network diagram, identify the critical path and its duration, determine the cost associated with the project using normal activity durations, and then recalculate the costs using shorter activity times.

Costs may vary according to the length of time taken for individual activities and also for the time taken by the project as a whole. For example, it may be possible to complete one activity in less time by hiring extra machinery at an extra cost, or by paying staff overtime rates to work longer days. Thus a shorter time leads to additional costs. The overall project may incur a penalty for overrunning its target completion date, or attract a bonus for early completion. In this instance, a shorter project time leads to less cost. It is a task of management to identify the optimum combination of time and cost to meet the requirements of a particular situation.

The process of reducing the overall project duration by applying increased resources to critical activities is called **crashing the network**, and hence we refer to **crash costs** and **crash times** in contrast to normal costs and normal times for activities.

Let's consider an example to illustrate the process of crashing a network.

The following activities are involved in completing a project:

Activity	Preceded by	Normal duration*	Normal cost £	Crash duration*	Crash cost £
A		4	200	3	300
B		5	100	2	220
C		4	40	3	50
D	A	3	200	3	200
E	D	4	130	1	280
F	A	6	30	2	230
G	B	7	80	5	140
H	E, F	4	60	2	180
			840		1,600

* weeks

All activities can be crashed one week at a time at the costs shown in the table. The project
manager wishes to know what the normal duration of the project will be, and also if it would be
cost-effective to complete the project in nine weeks. They have a budget of £1,500.

The first step is to draw the network diagram and identify the critical path and overall duration
using normal durations for each activity (see Figure 10.5).

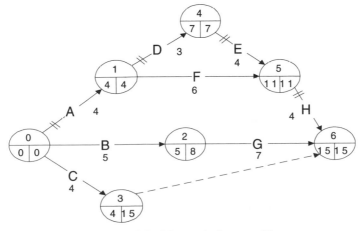

Figure 10.5   Network diagram (5)

The critical path is A, D, E, H, with a normal duration of 15 weeks. Total cost is £840 plus 15 weeks at £300 per week, a total of £5,340

Next, we need to identify the 'cost slope' for each activity and use this information to select the activities that should be crashed. Only activities on the critical path should be crashed, starting with the one that has the lowest cost slope. This can be calculated as:

$$\text{Cost slope} = \frac{\text{Crash cost} - \text{Normal cost}}{\text{Normal time} - \text{Crash time}}$$

> **Crucial concept** The **cost slope** is the cost associated with reducing an activity by one unit of time, assuming that the additional costs incurred are linear.

The cost slopes in this example are:

Activity	Cost slope*
A	100
B	40
C	10
D	–
E	50
F	50
G	30
H	60

* extra cost per week of crashing the activity

Activity C has the lowest cost slope, but it is not a critical activity. Activity E is the lowest cost slope for those activities that are on the critical path, so we should reduce the duration of this activity to its crash duration, i.e. to one day (see Figure 10.6). Costs will increase by £150 to £990, still within budget.

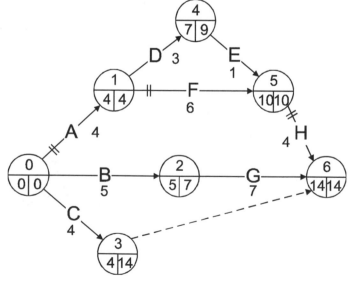

Figure 10.6   Network diagram (6)

The new critical path is A, F, H. The lowest cost slope here is activity F, which can be crashed by four weeks at a cost of £50 per week, increasing costs by £200 to £1,190. Again this gives us a revised network (see Figure 10.7).

> **Crucial tip**
>
> When you are crashing a network, you need to check at each stage whether the critical path has changed. As activities are reduced in duration, they can become non-critical, and a new critical path will need to be the focus of further amendments.

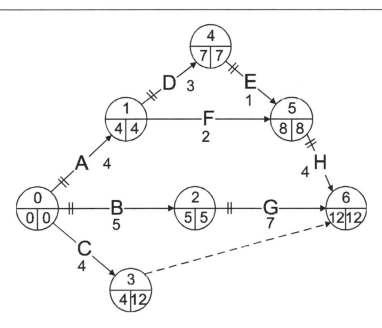

Figure 10.7   Network diagram (7)

In the revised network there are now two critical paths; B, G and A, D, E, H. To reduce the duration further, **both** paths need to be reduced together. Activity F has been reduced to its crash duration so it cannot be reduced further, and D has no scope for crashing at all. This leaves activities A and H on path A, D, E, H, and both activities on the path B, G. As we are dealing with two paths simultaneously, it is worth extracting the relevant information to ensure that we make the right choices in the next stage of crashing.

Activity	Normal duration	Crash duration	Cost slope £
A	4	3	100
H	4	2	60
B	5	2	40
G	7	5	30

The activities with the lowest cost slopes are H on path A, D, E, H and G on path B, G. Conveniently, they can both be reduced by two days. Costs will increase by a total of £180 to £1,370. The network now looks like Figure 10.8.

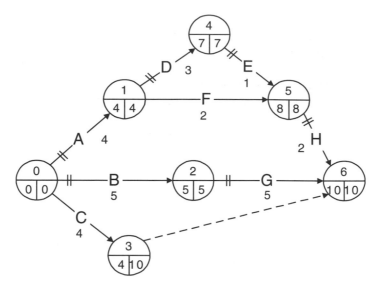

Figure 10.8   Network diagram (8)

The same two paths are still critical, so we can crash the remaining two activities, A and B. The final critical path is A, D, E, H, with a crash duration of nine weeks. We know this must be the final result (in terms of minimum duration) because all the activities on the path are at their crash durations, so there is no more scope for reducing the duration of the project. Additional costs will be £220, putting us over budget at £1,590. The network showing the minimum duration of nine weeks is given in Figure 10.9.

This result would imply that the project manager does not have the budget available to complete the project in nine weeks as the additional costs incurred through crashing have put the bill up to £1,590. However, in this process we have ended up with some activities at their crash costs and durations in the final network that are not on the critical path. This means paying extra to complete the activity in less time without it impacting on the overall duration of the project. So

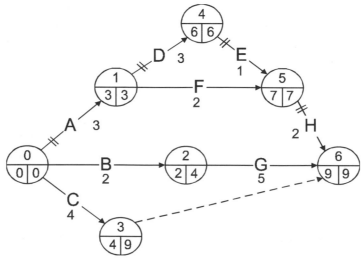

Figure 10.9   Network diagram (9)

we can amend the following activities by looking at the available float and 'uncrashing' where appropriate:

Activity	Cost slope	Float	Saving
B	40	2	80
G	30	2	60
F	50	2	100

B and G are on the same path, so we cannot uncrash both of them. Uncrashing B would save the larger amount, so the solution should be to uncrash B and F at a total saving of £180. This gives a total project cost of £1,410, which allows the project manager to plan for a project duration of nine weeks and still stay within budget.

> **Crucial tip**
>
> The process described above may seem very laborious and lengthy. We have gone through it in detail here because some questions require you to work out the cost at various different durations. If you just need to know the cost of the minimum duration, simply draw the network with all activities at their crash durations, and then uncrash any noncritical activities that have available float. Question 3 at the end of the chapter will give you practice in this.

Quick test

1. What is the formula for calculating the cost slope for an activity?
2. Why should you only crash activities that are on the critical path?

Section 5 — Probability and time estimates

What are you studying?
In the previous sections we looked at examples where the duration of an activity (both normal and crash) was given as a specific figure, e.g. 10 days. Times are not always so easily predicted, and in some cases it might be reasonable to assume a range of possible durations for an activity, each with an associated probability. In this section we look at ways of incorporating this into drawing and analysing networks.

How will you be assessed on this?
You may be expected to calculate expected durations for activities, based on probability estimates given in the question, and then to use these durations to produce network diagrams and carry out further analysis in the same way as we did in the previous sections.

The Project Evaluation and Review Technique (PERT) incorporates uncertainty into a formula for calculating the expected duration of an activity.

Crucial concept The **PERT** formula is calculated as:

$$\text{Estimated average duration} = \frac{\text{Optimistic time} + \text{Pessimistic time} + 4 \times \text{Most likely time}}{6}$$

Each activity of uncertain duration is assigned a probability distribution (either continuous or discrete), so that the probabilities of different durations for the whole project can be found. Where continuous distributions are used, it is usually assumed that they are normal distributions and that the durations of activities are independent of one another.

Example assuming continuous probabilities

Activity	Preceded by	Optimistic duration*	Most likely duration*	Pessimistic duration*
T		4	9	20
U		19	19	20
V	T	8	10	17
W	U	21	21	21
X	V	6	15	22
Y	X	7	11	20

*all durations are in days

Figure 10.10 shows the network diagram.

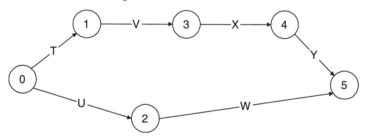

Figure 10.10   Network diagram (10)

Using the PERT formula we can work out expected durations for each activity and therefore the expected durations for the two paths.

Activity		Expected duration (days)
T	(4 + 36 + 20) / 6	10
U	(19 + 76 + 20) / 6	19.2
V	(8 + 40 + 17) / 6	10.8
W	(21 + 84 + 21) / 6	21
X	(6 + 60 + 22) / 6	14.7
Y	(7 + 44 + 20) / 6	11.8
Path T, V, X, Y	= 10 + 10.8 + 14.7 + 11.8 =	47.3
Path U, W	= 19.2 + 21 =	40.2

Therefore the critical path, based on expected durations, is T, V, X, Y with an expected duration of 47.3 days. You can see in this example that there is a very large variation in some of the activities, especially those on the critical path. If the actual times vary significantly from the expected durations, this can mean that a different path becomes critical, so managers will have to be aware of both the critical path and any other paths that are 'near critical' if the project is to be controlled effectively. In this example, if all the most optimistic times came into effect, path U, W would actually be the longest and therefore the critical path.

Example using discrete probabilities

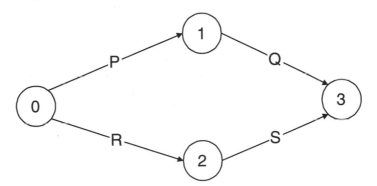

Figure 10.11   Network diagram (11)

Activity	Duration (weeks)	Probability
P	50	0.4
	60	0.6
Q	20	0.5
	30	0.5
R	30	0.8
	50	0.2
S	20	0.3
	40	0.7

The network diagram is shown in Figure 10.11.

We need to consider all the possible critical paths that could occur based on these probabilities. This is best done through a matrix that sets out all the combinations. For example, for path P, Q one possibility is that P takes 50 weeks and Q takes 20 weeks, a total of 70 weeks. This has a combined probability of 0.4 x 0.5 = 0.2. If that combination occurs along with durations of 30 for R and 20 for S, a total of 50 weeks, then P, Q will be the critical path as it is the longest. The probability of this being the case is found by multiplying the probability for each path, i.e. 0.2 x 0.24 = 0.048

Path	Duration	Probability	70	80	80	90
		Probability	0.2	0.3	0.2	0.3
	50	0.24	0.048 (70)	0.072 (80)	0.048 (80)	0.072 (90)
R,S	70	0.56	0.112 (70)	0.168 (80)	0.112 (80)	0.168 (80)
	70	0.06	0.012 (70)	0.018 (80)	0.012 (80)	0.018 (90)
	90	0.14	0.028 (70)	0.042 (90)	0.028 (90)	0.042 (90)

The figures in brackets indicate the critical path duration for each combination, and you can see that P, Q and R, S each become critical for different combinations. We can use this information to determine the probability of certain outcomes. For example, if we had a deadline that meant the project had to be completed in no more than 80 weeks, we can work out the probability of achieving that. All combinations in which the critical path has a duration of 70 or 80 weeks in the above matrix meet the deadline. So all we need do is either add up those probabilities, or as the probabilities all add up to 1 we can add up the probabilities for all combinations greater than 80 (as there are fewer) and subtract the result from 1.

0.18 + 0.028 + 0.042 + 0.028 + 0.042 = 0.32
1 − 0.32 = 0.68, so there is a 0.68 probability of meeting the deadline

Quick test

1. What is the PERT formula and how should it be used?

2. What is the expected duration of activity J if there is a 39% probability of it taking 3 days, otherwise it is expected to take 5.5 days?

   Is it 3.315, 4.525, or 5.075 days?

Answer to Quick test for Section 2
1. Total float   =   12

   Free float   =   6

   Independent float   =   5

Answer to Quick test for Section 5
2. 4.525 days

Crucial examples

1. A project is made up of the following activities:

Activity	Preceded by	Duration (days)
A		5
B	A	12
C	A	13
D	A	14
E	B	4
F	B, C, D	8
G	E	4

What is the critical path and the minimum time in which the project can be completed?

2. The following information relates to the installation of a new computer system for a purchasing function:

Activity	Description	Preceding activity	Duration (weeks)
A	Assess requirements		6
B	Initial training		6
C	Select software and hardware	A	8
D	Install system	C	2
E	Train operatives	B, D	12
F	Specific customer contacts	C	8
G	Order quantity standardisation	F	4
H	Coding	G	4
I	Prepare manuals	D, H	10
J	Initial debugging	D, H	4
K	Final training	E, I, J	6
L	Networking to other departments	K	20

(a) Draw the network and determine the overall completion time. Include the event numbers, EST and LSTs in the diagram.

(b) What is the critical path?

(c) What is the float for activity D?

3. Consider the network diagram in Figure 10.12.

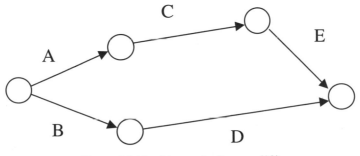

Figure 10.12   Network diagram (12)

Activity	Normal duration (weeks)	Crash duration (weeks)	Normal cost £	Crash cost £
A	6	4	10,000	2,000
B	4	3	5,000	3,000
C	3	2	4,000	1,000
D	8	6	9,000	1,500
E	7	4	7,000	333
			35,000	47,000

What is the minimum duration and the associated cost for the project. Note – it is not necessary to show the networks and costs at all possible durations.

4. Using the following information, determine the critical path for the project and the probability of completing it in no more than 3.5 months.

Activity	Preceding activity	Estimated time (months)	Probability
X		2	0.4
		2.5	0.6
Y	X	1	0.8
		1.5	0.2
Z		2	0.1
		3	0.5
		4	0.4

Answers

1. Critical path is A, D, dummy, F and the duration is 27 days.

2. (a) See Figure 10.13.

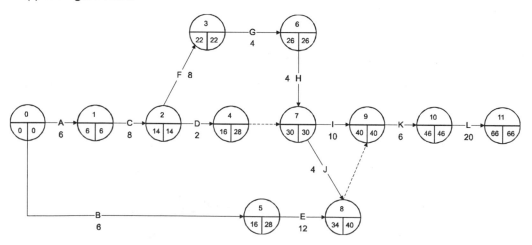

Figure 10.13   Network diagram (13)

(b) A, C, F, G, H, I, K, L

(c) Float = 28 – 14 – 2 = 12 weeks

3. Path A, C, E   = 4 + 2 + 4 = 10 days

   Path B, D   = 3 + 6 = 9 days

Float on activities B and D = 1 day. Uncrash B as this has the highest cost slope (£3,000 per day). Times and costs after crashing:

Activity	Duration	Cost £
A	4	14,000
B	4	5,000
C	2	5,000
D	6	12,000
E	4	8,000
		£44,000

4.

Path			X,Y			
	Duration		3	3.5	3.5	4
		Probability	0.32	0.08	0.48	0.12
	2	0.1	0.032	0.008	0.048	0.012
			(3)	(3.5)	(3.5)	(4)
Z	3	0.5	0.16	0.04	0.24	0.06
			(3)	(3.5)	(3.5)	(4)
	4	0.4	0.128	0.032	0.192	0.048
			(4)	(4)	(4)	(4)

Outcomes that meet the target of 3.5 months or less have probabilities of :

0.032 + 0.008 + 0.048 + 0.16 + 0.04 + 0.24 = 0.528

Crucial reading and research

Reading

The following texts provide further information and examples on network analysis:

Curwin, J. and Slater, R. (2002) *Quantitative Methods for Business Decisions*, 5th edn. Thomson Learning. Chapter 20: Networks (pp. 483–90 and 493–96).

Lucey, T. (1996) *Quantitative Techniques*, 5th edn. Letts Educational. See Chapter 22: Network Analysis – Introduction and Terminology (pp. 322–9), Chapter 23: Network Analysis – Time Analysis (pp. 330–42) and Chapter 24: Network Analysis – Cost Scheduling (pp. 343–7).

Research

Network analysis is a very practical technique, and you may be able to find examples of it in use in large organisations – particularly for planning large-scale tasks like construction or engineering projects. Seeing how the technique is used in practice can help you appreciate how it works and what it can achieve. You can even practise it by applying the technique to your own planning requirements, such as undertaking a large assignment as part of your studies, where activities, dates and dependencies are all involved.

You should also take a look at computer-based approaches to network analysis. The software Microsoft Project for Windows has all the elements of network analysis that we have covered in this chapter, and can create diagrams, identify the critical path, etc. quickly and accurately. But remember that in an examination you will be expected to do this without the aid of a computer, so don't use this software as an alternative to learning the technique in full.

A final point is that in this chapter we have been looking at activities and available time, assuming that if there is time available then the activity can be completed. In complex projects, as well as time there will be a need for other resources, such as personnel, equipment, vehicles, etc., and scheduling needs to take into account their availability. If you wish to look into this aspect of network analysis, the use of Gantt charts is covered in the texts mentioned above (i.e. Lucey: Chapter 25, and Curwin and Slater: Chapter 20.4).

EXAMINATION QUESTIONS
AND ANSWERS

Summary

The following questions are a further opportunity for you to test your learning. The suggested number of marks and time required for each question are for your guidance.

Questions

1. Tom Smith makes two types of toy, the Laura Doll and the Mary Doll. Each Laura Doll makes a contribution of £6 per unit and each Mary Doll £4.50. The resources used in producing the dolls, and the amount available per week are as follows:

	Laura Doll	Mary Doll	Maximum
Machine hours	3	6	150
Labour hours	9	6	270
Material (kg)	1.5	1.5	60

Market research indicates that the most number of Mary Dolls that could be sold in a week is 20, and Tom does not wish to build up additional stocks.

(a) State the various constraints in an appropriate format. 6

(b) What is the objective function, assuming the Tom wishes to maximise contribution? 2

(c) Solve the problem using a graph and simultaneous equations to identify the maximum contribution. 8

(d) How would the solution be affected if the machine hours availability increased to 180 hours? 4

Total: 20 marks
Suggested time: 40 minutes

2. Prosim Ltd have set up a project team to manage the installation of a new payroll and personnel system. The project manager has identified the main activities involved and their estimated duration (days).

Activity	Preceding activity	Required time	Crash time	Crash cost £
A		4	2	850
B	A	6	4	900
C	A	8	5	1,350
D	A	3	3	
E	B	5	5	
F	C	9	9	
G	D	11	7	1,550
H	D	15	11	1,800
I	F	8	6	3,000
J	E	7	5	750
K	J	10	7	930
L	G, I	13	9	2,000
M	H	7	5	700
N	K, L	9	7	750
O	N	1	1	

a) Draw the network, and identify the duration of the critical path. 8

b) Explain how you would use the crash time information to reduce the critical path if the deadline for the new system meant that it had to be completed within 48 days. 7

Total: 15 marks
Suggested time: 30 minutes

3. King Builders are considering the purchase of a piece of land for £120,000. The land has planning permission to build two houses. The cost of building the two properties will depend on weather conditions, and the following estimates have been put together by Mr King:

Weather conditions	Probability	Building costs
Wet	20%	£280,000
Average	40%	£240,000
Good	40%	£200,000

Mr King has also estimated the selling prices for each house, depending on market conditions:

Static	30%	£160,000
Slow increase	40%	£200,000
Rapid increase	30%	£230,000

If Mr King decides to go ahead with the project, he will need to set aside £400,000 in a current account and earn no interest on the money for the three months that the project is expected to take. If he does not go ahead with it, he can invest it at a rate of 4% per annum.

(a) What is the expected value of the building programme? 10

(b) Explain how Mr King should use this information in deciding whether to go ahead with the project or not. 5

Total: 15 marks
Suggested time: 30 minutes

4. A company wishes to decide whether to introduce a new procedure into its manufacturing operation. To help it decide two test assembly lines set up and separate groups of employees trained in the new and existing procedures. Once trained the output of each group was measured over a two week period and the length of time for each employee to complete the new procedure was measured, with the following results:

Team A		Team B	
32	88	105	80
111	35	98	60
35	93	107	64
56	102	61	62
123	119	34	73

(a) Does this data give us any reason to believe that the new procedure (worked on by Team B) is any faster than the old one? 12

(b) If the company had available to it data relating to the performance of 50 employees in each team would this have changed your approach to the conduct of the test? 2

(c) You are asked by the training manager of the company involved to explain how you are able to draw the conclusion that you have done based on such small amounts of data. Explain in a way that a non-expert would understand. 6

Total: 20 marks
Suggested time: 30 minutes

5. (a) A manufacturing company has three plants located around the country. Data on error rates, classified according to type of error, is collected. The group operations manager asks

you to analyse the data to determine whether there is any statistical evidence to support the view that error rates vary from plant to plant. Using an appropriate test you are required to determine whether or not there is any association between plant location and error rates. The data is as follows:

Observed values

| | | Error type | | | |
		I	II	III	IV
Plant	A	17	24	52	15
	B	30	36	39	6
	C	38	20	56	23

10

(b) One of the plants involved in the analysis of error rates makes *Veljoen*, a chemical used in the nuclear processing industry to catalyse the reaction process. Scientists at the plant have formed a hypothesis that there is a connection between the viscosity of batches of *Veljoen* produced and the efficiency with which the catalytic effect takes place. Data from a number of batches are gathered as follows:

Viscosity	Efficiency
74.02	44.11
34.58	14.34
65.52	90.82
95.33	81.74
77.14	47.36
32.11	18.93
96.90	90.43
73.55	0.96
47.18	1.11

Is there any evidence to support the scientists' view that there is a connection between viscosity and efficiency as measured by the sample data above?

10

(c) From the data presented in part (b) of this question estimate the efficiency of *Veljoen* with a viscosity of 90 units.

5

Total: 25 marks
Suggested time: 45 minutes

Answers

Answer 1
(a) 3L + 6M $\leq$ 150 (machine hours)

9L + 6M $\leq$ 270 (labour hours)

1.5L + 1.5M $\leq$ 60 (materials)

M $\leq$ 20 (sales)

(b) Maximise 6L + 4.5M

(c) Graph shows the objective function will be maximise where the machine and labour constraints meet. Solving these equations:

$$3L + 6M = 150 \text{ (machine hours)}$$
$$9L + 6M = 270 \text{ (labour hours)}$$
$$6L = 120$$
$$L = 20$$

Substituting in machine hours equation:

$$60 + 6M = 150$$
$$M = 15$$

Contribution = $(20 \times 6) + (15 \times 4.5) = £187.5$

(d) As the line for the machine hours constraint moves out, the objective function would now be maximised where labour hours and sales constraints meet. We know, therefore, that M must be 20, so this can be substituted in the labour hours constraint:

$$9L + 6M = 270$$
$$9L + 120 = 270$$
$$9L = 150$$
$$L = 16.67$$

As it is only practical to make whole dolls, the production over a single week should be 16 Laura Dolls and 20 Mary Dolls, but over a longer period it may be possible to plan for making an average of 16.67 Mary Dolls each week. The contribution at this new level will be $(16 \times 6) + (20 \times 4.5) = £186$.

Answer 2

(a) The critical path is A, C, F, I, L, N, O with a duration of 52 days.

(b) The first step would be to calculate the cost slope for each activity, which highlights which activities can be reduced most cost-effectively. Activities with the lowest cost slopes on the critical path can then be reduced, checking at each stage whether a different path becomes critical. In this example, the next longest path is 42 days, so we can reduce the critical path to 45 without making any other activities critical.

The order in which the activities would be reduced is:

Activity	Cost slope	Possible reduction	Cost
N	£375	2 days	£750
A	£425	2 days	£850
C	£450	3 days	£1,350

This will give the required seven-day reduction at a total cost of £2,950.

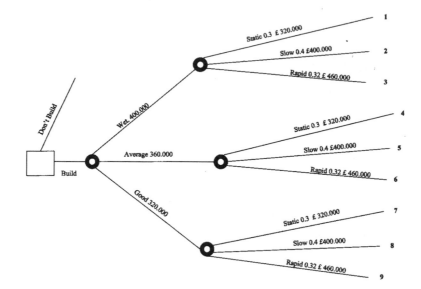

Figure A.1   Basic decision tree structure

Answer 3

(a) The basic decision tree structure is given in Figure A.1.

	Income less costs	Probability	EV
1	(80,000)	0.06	(4,800)
2	0	0.08	0
3	60,000	0.06	3,600
4	(40,000)	0.12	(4,800)
5	40,000	0.16	6,400
6	100,000	0.12	12,000
7	0	0.12	0
8	80,000	0.16	12,800
9	140,000	0.12	16,800
	EV for 'Build'		42,000
	EV for 'Don't build'		16,000

(b) The positive expected value of £42,000 for the 'Build' branch of the tree means that the project can give a return that is higher than investing the money at 4% interest. However, there are many things that might affect this simple interpretation:

- The EV of £42,000 is not actually a possible outcome – it is the theoretical outcome of carrying out the project many times.

- Two of the outcomes are a loss, the higher being £80,000.

- Are the probability estimates reliable?

- Are there some outcomes not included (e.g. falling house prices)?

- Are the cost estimates accurate?

- Is Mr King risk-averse, neutral or risk-seeking? He may prefer the certainty of £16,000 rather than the theoretical possibility of £42,000.

From this we can see that the Pearson product-moment coefficient of correlation is 0.6823. This tells us that increases in viscosity are associated with increases in efficiency as a catalyst. However, the coefficient is not large, which suggests a weak association at best. Calculating the coefficient of determination, which is 0.4655, shows us that less than half of the variation in catalytic efficiency is explained by variations in viscosity. We might advise our scientists to go back to the drawing board.

(c) We can use the calculations that we have already done to determine the coefficients of the least squares regression line which we need to make our prediction.

$$y = a + bx$$

$$b = \frac{S_{xy}}{S_{xx}}$$

$$a = \overline{y} - b\overline{x}$$

Therefore $b = 4,822.73 / 4,550.19 = 1.0599$. Substituting this into the final equation gives $a = 43.31 - (1.0599 \times 66.26) = -26.9190$ so $y = -26.9190 + 1.0599x$.

Substituting $x = 90$ into this equation gives $y = 41.5530$.

- Are there other opportunities for investing the money – e.g. purchasing shares?
- And so on.

Question 4

(a) Let's set out the hypotheses first of all. We are asked about the evidence to support the view that the new procedure is quicker than the old one. This suggests a one-tailed test, and therefore null and alternative hypotheses as follows:

$$H_0 : \mu_1 - \mu_2 = 0$$
$$H_a : \mu_1 - \mu_2 \neq 0$$

We need to do some preliminary work here since we haven't been given the sample standard deviation for each sample, which we'll need to calculate s.

x_i	$x_i - \overline{x}$	$(x_i - \overline{x})^2$	$(x_i - \overline{x})^2 / n$	y_i	$y_i - \overline{y}$	$(y_i - \overline{y})^2$	$(y_i - \overline{y})^2 / n$
32	−47.4	2246.8	224.7	105	30.6	936.4	93.6
111	31.6	998.6	99.9	98	23.6	557.0	55.7
35	−44.4	1971.4	197.1	107	32.6	1062.8	106.3
56	−23.4	547.6	54.8	61	−13.4	179.6	18.0
123	43.6	1901.0	190.1	34	−40.4	1632.2	163.2
88	8.6	74.0	7.4	80	5.6	31.4	3.1
35	−44.4	1971.4	197.1	60	−14.4	207.4	20.7
93	13.6	185.0	18.5	64	−10.4	108.2	10.8
102	22.6	510.8	51.1	62	−12.4	153.8	15.4
119	39.6	1568.2	156.8	73	−1.4	2.0	0.2
Mean 79.4				74.4			
Sum			1,197.4				487.0
SD			34.604				22.069

As you can see from these calculations, the sample standard deviations turn out to be 34.604 and 22.069 respectively, with means of 79.4 and 74.4.

We may now calculate the pooled estimate of the population standard error:

$$s^2 = \frac{(n_1 - 1)s_1^2 + (n_2 - 1)s_2^2}{(n_1 - 1) + (n_2 - 1)}$$

$$= \frac{9 \times 34.604^2 + 9 \times 22.069^2}{18}$$

$$= 842.2387$$

We need the square root of this to use in the formula for the test statistic: it is 29.02.

We can now therefore calculate the value of the test statistic, t, as:

$$t = \frac{(\overline{x}_1 - \overline{x}_2) - D_0}{s\sqrt{\frac{1}{n_1} + \frac{1}{n_2}}}$$

$$= \frac{79.4 - 74.4 - 0}{29.02\sqrt{0.2}}$$

$$= 0.385$$

It is almost unnecessary to look up the critical value of the test statistic but we'll do it anyway. From tables the one-tailed value of t with 18 degrees of freedom at the 5% level is 1.734. Our calculated value is clearly much less than this and therefore we have no grounds to reject the null hypothesis.

(b) If the company had data relating to 50 employees then this would have allowed us to use the z-statistic as the test statistic, since the sample would have been large. However, we could equally have used the t-test: it's not wrong to do that but probably unnecessary and a little more complicated given that we need to take into account the issue of degrees of freedom.

(c) The data that we used to do our analysis was drawn at random. Statistical theory tells us that in these circumstances our sample statistics, in particular the sample mean and the sample standard deviation, are good estimates of the true values in the population. We are therefore justified in using the sample data as the basis for our estimates of the population values.

We started our analysis by assuming that there was no difference between the two methods. This is rather like assuming innocence until there is proof of guilt. It places the burden on the 'prosecutor' (here the person conducting the test) to demonstrate 'beyond all reasonable doubt' that the results do not support the initial view that there is no difference. If we cannot produce evidence to reject the starting assumption (the null hypothesis) then we cannot 'convict'. As in a court of law, the accused is judged to be guilty or not guilty: we do not expect a jury to return a verdict of innocent, nor do we do so when we carry out a test like this.

We determine whether or not we can reject the null hypothesis by calculating a 'test statistic'. This is designed to be compared with values from tables that allow us to make our decision, to reject the null hypothesis or not, with a stated degree of confidence. When we do this we determine in advance the probability that we will reject the null hypothesis when we ought not to do so. In this way we can control the maximum error with known probability.

In this case the calculated value of our test statistic was very much less than the critical value that would have allowed us to reject the null hypothesis. We therefore have no statistical reason to do so and therefore cannot conclude that there is any association between the two training methods and the output of the two groups.

Question 5

(a) The question calls for a chi-squared test of association. We calculate the value of the test statistic as follows:

Observed values:

		I	II	III	IV	
				Error type		
Plant	A	17	24	52	15	108
	B	30	36	39	6	111
	C	38	20	56	23	137
		85	80	147	44	356

Expected values:

	I	II	III	IV	
			Error type		
Plant	25.79	24.27	44.60	13.35	108
	26.50	24.94	45.83	13.72	111
	32.71	30.79	56.57	16.93	137
	85	80	147	44	356

Calculations $(O - E)^2/E$:

I	II	III	IV
		Error type	
2.9959	0.003	1.2278	0.2039
0.4623	4.9047	1.0179	4.3439
0.8555	3.7812	0.0057	2.1763

Calculated chi square value 21.978

We need to decide on a confidence level – 95% is common and so we will use that. We also need to determine the number of degrees of freedom. There are four columns and four rows and so there are 6 i.e. $(4-1) \times (3-1)$, degrees of freedom. From tables we see that the critical value of the chi-squared statistic at this level with 6 degrees of freedom is 12.592. Our calculated value of 21.978 is much larger than this and therefore we may reject the null hypothesis in favour of the belief that error rates do vary significantly from plant to plant.

(b) You are required to calculate either or both of the Pearson product-moment correlation coefficient and the coefficient of determination. The calculations should be set out as follows:

x	y	xy	x^2	y^2
74.02	44.11	3,265.51	5,479.38	1,946.13
34.58	14.34	495.89	1,195.66	205.67
65.52	90.82	5,950.71	4,292.84	8,248.85
95.33	81.74	7,792.36	9,088.29	6,681.22
77.14	47.36	3,653.42	5,951.12	2,242.86
32.11	18.93	607.81	1,031.35	358.21
96.90	90.43	8,763.19	9,389.89	8,178.31
73.55	0.96	70.60	5,410.28	0.92
47.18	1.11	52.48	2,226.19	1.24
$\sum$ 596.35	389.81	30,651.97	44,065.00	27,863.39
Mean 66.26	43.31			

Substituting into the formulae gives:

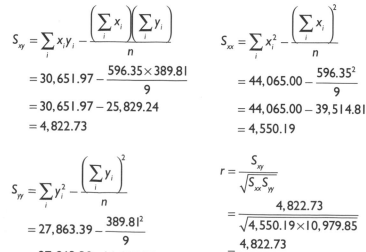

$$S_{xy} = \sum_i x_i y_i - \frac{\left(\sum_i x_i\right)\left(\sum_i y_i\right)}{n}$$

$$= 30,651.97 - \frac{596.35 \times 389.81}{9}$$

$$= 30,651.97 - 25,829.24$$

$$= 4,822.73$$

$$S_{xx} = \sum_i x_i^2 - \frac{\left(\sum_i x_i\right)^2}{n}$$

$$= 44,065.00 - \frac{596.35^2}{9}$$

$$= 44,065.00 - 39,514.81$$

$$= 4,550.19$$

$$S_{yy} = \sum_i y_i^2 - \frac{\left(\sum_i y_i\right)^2}{n}$$

$$= 27,863.39 - \frac{389.81^2}{9}$$

$$= 27,863.39 - 16,883.54$$

$$= 10,979.85$$

$$r = \frac{S_{xy}}{\sqrt{S_{xx}S_{yy}}}$$

$$= \frac{4,822.73}{\sqrt{4,550.19 \times 10,979.85}}$$

$$= \frac{4,822.73}{7,068.27}$$

$$= 0.6823$$

INDEX

- Are there other opportunities for investing the money – e.g. purchasing shares?
- And so on.

Question 4

(a) Let's set out the hypotheses first of all. We are asked about the evidence to support the view that the new procedure is quicker than the old one. This suggests a one-tailed test, and therefore null and alternative hypotheses as follows:

$$H_0 : \mu_1 - \mu_2 = 0$$
$$H_a : \mu_1 - \mu_2 \neq 0$$

We need to do some preliminary work here since we haven't been given the sample standard deviation for each sample, which we'll need to calculate s.

x_i	$x_i - \bar{x}$	$(x_i - \bar{x})^2$	$(x_i - \bar{x})^2 / n$	y_i	$y_i - \bar{y}$	$(y_i - \bar{y})^2$	$(y_i - \bar{y})^2 / n$
32	−47.4	2246.8	224.7	105	30.6	936.4	93.6
111	31.6	998.6	99.9	98	23.6	557.0	55.7
35	−44.4	1971.4	197.1	107	32.6	1062.8	106.3
56	−23.4	547.6	54.8	61	−13.4	179.6	18.0
123	43.6	1901.0	190.1	34	−40.4	1632.2	163.2
88	8.6	74.0	7.4	80	5.6	31.4	3.1
35	−44.4	1971.4	197.1	60	−14.4	207.4	20.7
93	13.6	185.0	18.5	64	−10.4	108.2	10.8
102	22.6	510.8	51.1	62	−12.4	153.8	15.4
119	39.6	1568.2	156.8	73	−1.4	2.0	0.2
Mean 79.4				74.4			
Sum			1,197.4				487.0
SD			34.604				22.069

As you can see from these calculations, the sample standard deviations turn out to be 34.604 and 22.069 respectively, with means of 79.4 and 74.4.

We may now calculate the pooled estimate of the population standard error:

$$s^2 = \frac{(n_1 - 1)s_1^2 + (n_2 - 1)s_2^2}{(n_1 - 1) + (n_2 - 1)}$$

$$= \frac{9 \times 34.604^2 + 9 \times 22.069^2}{18}$$

$$= 842.2387$$

We need the square root of this to use in the formula for the test statistic: it is 29.02.

We can now therefore calculate the value of the test statistic, t, as:

$$t = \frac{(\bar{x}_1 - \bar{x}_2) - D_0}{s\sqrt{\dfrac{1}{n_1} + \dfrac{1}{n_2}}}$$

$$= \frac{79.4 - 74.4 - 0}{29.02\sqrt{0.2}}$$

$$= 0.385$$

It is almost unnecessary to look up the critical value of the test statistic but we'll do it anyway. From tables the one-tailed value of t with 18 degrees of freedom at the 5% level is 1.734. Our calculated value is clearly much less than this and therefore we have no grounds to reject the null hypothesis.

(b) If the company had data relating to 50 employees then this would have allowed us to use the z-statistic as the test statistic, since the sample would have been large. However, we could equally have used the t-test: it's not wrong to do that but probably unnecessary and a little more complicated given that we need to take into account the issue of degrees of freedom.

(c) The data that we used to do our analysis was drawn at random. Statistical theory tells us that in these circumstances our sample statistics, in particular the sample mean and the sample standard deviation, are good estimates of the true values in the population. We are therefore justified in using the sample data as the basis for our estimates of the population values.

We started our analysis by assuming that there was no difference between the two methods. This is rather like assuming innocence until there is proof of guilt. It places the burden on the 'prosecutor' (here the person conducting the test) to demonstrate 'beyond all reasonable doubt' that the results do not support the initial view that there is no difference. If we cannot produce evidence to reject the starting assumption (the null hypothesis) then we cannot 'convict'. As in a court of law, the accused is judged to be guilty or not guilty: we do not expect a jury to return a verdict of innocent, nor do we do so when we carry out a test like this.

We determine whether or not we can reject the null hypothesis by calculating a 'test statistic'. This is designed to be compared with values from tables that allow us to make our decision, to reject the null hypothesis or not, with a stated degree of confidence. When we do this we determine in advance the probability that we will reject the null hypothesis when we ought not to do so. In this way we can control the maximum error with known probability.

In this case the calculated value of our test statistic was very much less than the critical value that would have allowed us to reject the null hypothesis. We therefore have no statistical reason to do so and therefore cannot conclude that there is any association between the two training methods and the output of the two groups.

Question 5

(a) The question calls for a chi-squared test of association. We calculate the value of the test statistic as follows:

Observed values:

		I	II	III	IV	
				Error type		
Plant	A	17	24	52	15	108
	B	30	36	39	6	111
	C	38	20	56	23	137
		85	80	147	44	356

Expected values:

	I	II	III	IV	
			Error type		
Plant	25.79	24.27	44.60	13.35	108
	26.50	24.94	45.83	13.72	111
	32.71	30.79	56.57	16.93	137
	85	80	147	44	356

Calculations $(O - E)^2/E$:

	Error type		
I	II	III	IV
2.9959	0.003	1.2278	0.2039
0.4623	4.9047	1.0179	4.3439
0.8555	3.7812	0.0057	2.1763

Calculated chi square value   21.978

We need to decide on a confidence level – 95% is common and so we will use that. We also need to determine the number of degrees of freedom. There are four columns and four rows and so there are 6 i.e. $(4 - 1) \times (3 - 1)$, degrees of freedom. From tables we see that the critical value of the chi-squared statistic at this level with 6 degrees of freedom is 12.592. Our calculated value of 21.978 is much larger than this and therefore we may reject the null hypothesis in favour of the belief that error rates do vary significantly from plant to plant.

(b) You are required to calculate either or both of the Pearson product-moment correlation coefficient and the coefficient of determination. The calculations should be set out as follows:

x	y	xy	x^2	y^2
74.02	44.11	3,265.51	5,479.38	1,946.13
34.58	14.34	495.89	1,195.66	205.67
65.52	90.82	5,950.71	4,292.84	8,248.85
95.33	81.74	7,792.36	9,088.29	6,681.22
77.14	47.36	3,653.42	5,951.12	2,242.86
32.11	18.93	607.81	1,031.35	358.21
96.90	90.43	8,763.19	9,389.89	8,178.31
73.55	0.96	70.60	5,410.28	0.92
47.18	1.11	52.48	2,226.19	1.24
$\sum$ 596.35	389.81	30,651.97	44,065.00	27,863.39
Mean 66.26	43.31			

Substituting into the formulae gives:

$$S_{xy} = \sum_i x_i y_i - \frac{\left(\sum_i x_i\right)\left(\sum_i y_i\right)}{n}$$

$$= 30,651.97 - \frac{596.35 \times 389.81}{9}$$

$$= 30,651.97 - 25,829.24$$

$$= 4,822.73$$

$$S_{xx} = \sum_i x_i^2 - \frac{\left(\sum_i x_i\right)^2}{n}$$

$$= 44,065.00 - \frac{596.35^2}{9}$$

$$= 44,065.00 - 39,514.81$$

$$= 4,550.19$$

$$S_{yy} = \sum_i y_i^2 - \frac{\left(\sum_i y_i\right)^2}{n}$$

$$= 27,863.39 - \frac{389.81^2}{9}$$

$$= 27,863.39 - 16,883.54$$

$$= 10,979.85$$

$$r = \frac{S_{xy}}{\sqrt{S_{xx} S_{yy}}}$$

$$= \frac{4,822.73}{\sqrt{4,550.19 \times 10,979.85}}$$

$$= \frac{4,822.73}{7,068.27}$$

$$= 0.6823$$

From this we can see that the Pearson product-moment coefficient of correlation is 0.6823. This tells us that increases in viscosity are associated with increases in efficiency as a catalyst. However, the coefficient is not large, which suggests a weak association at best. Calculating the coefficient of determination, which is 0.4655, shows us that less than half of the variation in catalytic efficiency is explained by variations in viscosity. We might advise our scientists to go back to the drawing board.

(c) We can use the calculations that we have already done to determine the coefficients of the least squares regression line which we need to make our prediction.

$$y = a + bx$$

$$b = \frac{S_{xy}}{S_{xx}}$$

$$a = \overline{y} - b\overline{x}$$

Therefore $b = 4{,}822.73 / 4{,}550.19 = 1.0599$. Substituting this into the final equation gives $a = 43.31 - (1.0599 \times 66.26) = -26.9190$ so $y = -26.9190 + 1.0599x$.

Substituting $x = 90$ into this equation gives $y = 41.5530$.

INDEX